easy breakfast & brunch

easy breakfast & brunch

simple recipes for morning treats

RYLAND
PETERS
& SMALL

LONDON NEW YORK

Designer Iona Hoyle
Editor Céline Hughes
Picture Research Emily Westlake
Production Gemma Moules
Publishing Director Alison Starling

Indexer Sandra Shotter

First published in Great Britain in 2007
by Ryland Peters & Small
20–21 Jockey's Fields
London WC1R 4BW
www.rylandpeters.com

10 9 8 7 6 5 4 3 2 1

Text © Susannah Blake, Celia Brooks
Brown, Maxine Clark, Linda Collister,
Clare Ferguson, Brian Glover, Clare
Gordon-Smith, Kate Habershon,
Rachael Anne Hill, Jennifer Joyce,
Annie Nichols, Jane Noraika, Louise
Pickford, Ben Reed, Jennie Shapter,
Fran Warde, Lindy Wildsmith, and
Ryland Peters & Small 2007

Design and photographs
© Ryland Peters & Small 2007

Printed in China

ISBN 978 1 84597 484 8

A CIP record for this book is available
from the British Library.

Notes

• All spoon measurements are level
unless otherwise specified.

• Uncooked or partly cooked eggs
should not be served to the very
young, the very old, those with
compromised immune systems or
to pregnant women.

• To sterilize preserving jars, wash
them in hot, soapy water and rinse
in boiling water. Place in a large pan,
then cover with hot water. With the
saucepan lid on, bring the water to
the boil and continue boiling for
15 minutes. Turn off the heat, then
leave the jars in the hot water until just
before they are to be filled. Sterilize
the lids for 5 minutes, by boiling,
or according to the manufacturer's
instructions. Jars should be filled and
sealed while they are still hot.

contents

introduction

It is well documented that breakfast is the most important meal of the day but many of us fall into the trap of being in too much of a hurry to eat or drink anything as we fly out of the door to start the day. A look through the tempting range and diversity of recipes in this book could help to change all that.

There are dishes here to satisfy any number of tastes and circumstances. For those who are time-poor first thing in the morning, fruit is the ideal way to go, whether in the form of a nutritious smoothie or a scrumptious compote enlivening a bowl of homemade muesli. Baked goods are a winner any time. Many of the recipes keep for several days and freeze well, so even if you are on the run, you can take them along as a packed breakfast.

Weekends, holidays, sleep-overs and house-parties provide the perfect excuse for blurring the boundaries between breakfast and lunch. The socializing opportunities a breakfast or brunch get-together offers are second-to-none: the atmosphere is decidedly relaxed and informal, and its timing allows everyone to head off to different activities satiated and energized, and still with much of the day free.

Wherever possible, use fresh seasonal ingredients. Above all, be inspired and enjoy the preparation of these delicious recipes – it is easy to underestimate the uplifting effect that taking the time to cook for those closest to us, or even simply for oneself, can have.

fruit & oats

There's no better way to preserve the lusciousness of fruit than in a compote – and it's so easy to do. You can use any seasonal ripe fruit and it's lovely to have it all year round with muesli, porridge or yoghurt. Compote is also great served as a simple and light dessert after a rich meal. Experiment with combinations of your favourite fruits to make your own particular blend.

winter dried fruit pot

150 g dried apricots, stoned

150 g dates, stoned

150 g prunes, stoned

150 g sultanas

150 g dried blueberries

60 g molasses sugar

serves 6

Put all the ingredients in a saucepan, add just enough water to cover and stir. Cover with a lid, bring to the boil and simmer for 30 minutes. Leave to cool, then transfer to a storage jar with a tight-fitting lid and refrigerate until needed.

rhubarb & plum compote

400 g rhubarb, chopped

400 g plums, stoned

2 cm fresh ginger, peeled and thinly sliced

75 g sugar

serves 6

Put all the ingredients in a saucepan with 75 ml water, cover with a lid and bring to the boil. Lower the heat and simmer for 5 minutes. Leave the lid on and set aside to cool. Transfer to a storage jar with a tight-fitting lid and refrigerate until needed.

apple & pear compote

500 g apples, peeled, cored and chopped

500 g pears, peeled, cored and chopped

60 g light brown sugar

1 vanilla pod, split lengthways

serves 6

Put the fruit in a saucepan with 50 ml water, then add the sugar and vanilla pod. Stir, cover with a lid and bring to the boil. Lower the heat and simmer for 5 minutes. Leave the lid on and set aside to cool. Transfer to a storage jar with a tight-fitting lid and refrigerate until needed.

This is a simple fruit compote that is best served slightly warm. You can use nectarines instead of peaches if you prefer, plus whatever berries you fancy. It is complemented by thick, Greek yoghurt and can even be served as a healthy dessert.

warm compote
with peaches, apricots & blueberries

2 unwaxed oranges

3 ripe peaches, stoned and sliced

8–12 apricots, stoned and halved

175 g blueberries

25 g caster sugar

1 cinnamon stick

Greek yoghurt, to serve

serves 4

Peel the zest from 1 of the oranges, removing only the zest and not the bitter white pith. Cut the zest into thin strips and put in a shallow saucepan. Squeeze the juice from both oranges and add to the pan.

Add the peaches, apricots, blueberries, sugar and cinnamon stick to the pan and heat gently until the sugar dissolves. Cover and simmer gently for 4–5 minutes, or until the fruits are softened.

Serve the compote warm with Greek yoghurt.

There isn't much to beat figs straight from the tree, bursting with sweetness and a sublime flavour. Try to buy figs as ripe as possible for this dish. If they are unavailable, use other fruits such as peaches, apricots or cherries.

fresh figs
with ricotta & honeycomb

500 g fresh ripe figs (about 8)

500 g ricotta cheese, sliced

**a piece of honeycomb or
4–8 tablespoons honey**

serves 4

Arrange the figs and ricotta on a large plate and serve the honeycomb or honey in a separate bowl for everyone to help themselves.

Sometimes the best meals are the simplest – just fantastic fresh ingredients thrown together in no time. Everyone loves fruit, especially if it's all been prepared for them and looks stunning. This one is always a brunch winner.

fruit platter

1 ripe melon, such as orange cantaloupe or green honeydew

2 papayas

freshly squeezed juice of 2 limes

300 g mixed berries, such as blackberries, blueberries, raspberries, redcurrants and strawberries

honey yoghurt

450 ml Greek yoghurt

6 tablespoons clear honey

serves 4

Peel, halve and deseed the melon, then cut into wedges and slice. Divide between 4 plates. Peel, halve, deseed and cut the papaya into wedges. Add to the melon. Sprinkle with the lime juice, then add the berries.

Dollop the yoghurt next to the fruit and drizzle with the honey.

Calcium is vital for healthy teeth and bones, and eating yoghurt is a great way of getting enough. Teaming yoghurt with fresh fruit is an ideal way to start the day. Look into making your own in a special yoghurt machine if you want to avoid shop-bought varieties which often contain added sugar.

plum & honey cup

500 g plums, stoned

2 tablespoons honey

200 g natural bio yoghurt

200 g mascarpone cheese

serves 4

Put the plums in a saucepan with the honey and 50 ml water. Bring to the boil over medium heat, then cover and simmer very gently for about 8 minutes. Set aside to cool.

Mix the yoghurt and mascarpone together. Half-fill 4 glasses with this, then top with the cooked plums.

frozen berry yoghurt cup

500 g frozen mixed berries

100 g unrefined caster sugar

400 g Greek yoghurt

serves 4

Put the frozen berries in a blender with the sugar and blitz into small pieces. Take 4 glasses and fill with alternating layers of yoghurt and berries. Set aside for 5 minutes before serving.

banana & granola yoghurt pot

400 g natural bio yoghurt

3 ripe bananas, sliced

50 g pecans, roughly chopped

75 g molasses sugar

100 g House Granola (page 29)

50 g chocolate, grated

serves 4

Divide the yoghurt between 4 glasses. Top with the bananas, then add the pecans, sugar, granola and chocolate.

Vanilla sugar is easy to make – just put a couple of vanilla pods in a jar of sugar and leave them there, topping up with fresh sugar as necessary. You can use the pods for cooking, pat dry with kitchen paper, then return them to the sugar.

roasted mascarpone peaches

4 large, ripe peaches

2 tablespoons clear honey

150 g mascarpone cheese

3 tablespoons vanilla sugar

1 vanilla pod, split lengthways (optional)

1 tablespoon freshly squeezed lemon juice

serves 4

Preheat the oven to 200°C (400°F) Gas 6.

Cut the peaches in half, remove the stones and arrange cut-side up in a roasting tin. Pour over the honey and bake in the preheated oven for about 20 minutes, or until softened and lightly golden.

Mix the mascarpone with the vanilla sugar and lemon juice. (If you want a stronger vanilla flavour, scrape the seeds from a vanilla pod into the mascarpone.) Spoon onto the hot peaches and serve.

Keep a big bowl of this compote in the refrigerator – it keeps well and is great with yoghurt and a sprinkling of seeds. With lighter teas, use lighter-flavoured fruits such as peaches and apples and flavour with lemon zest. Use orange zest to flavour stronger teas, together with stronger spices such as star anise. There is no need to add sugar, because the natural sugars from the fruits thicken the syrup as it cooks.

tea-infused
fruit compote

2 teaspoons leaf tea, such as Earl Grey or jasmine

500 g mixed dried fruit, such as prunes, apricots or figs

300 ml apple juice

2 crushed cardamom pods

1 cinnamon stick

grated zest of 1 unwaxed orange

serves 4

Make a large pot of tea with the leaf tea and 1 litre boiling water and set aside to brew. Put the fruit in a bowl and completely cover with the brewed tea. Cover and let soak for several hours or overnight.

Transfer to a saucepan, then add the apple juice, cardamom pods, cinnamon stick and orange zest. Bring slowly to the boil, then reduce the heat and simmer for about 20 minutes until soft. Remove all the spices and leave to cool.

Cover and refrigerate for up to 1 week.

These kebabs are a great alternative to fruit salad. They work just as well cooked on a barbecue and served as a dessert in the summer. Feel free to experiment using your favourite fruits to get just the taste you like.

kickstart kebabs

2 small bananas, sliced

freshly squeezed juice of 1 lemon

8 cubes of tinned pineapple in fruit juice, drained

1 large orange, peeled and divided into segments

8 prunes, stoned

8 dried apricots

2 tablespoons freshly squeezed orange juice

1 tablespoon clear honey

½ teaspoon ground mixed spice

low-fat natural yoghurt, to serve

4 long wooden skewers, soaked in water for 10 minutes

makes 4 kebabs

Put the bananas in a shallow bowl, sprinkle with the lemon juice and toss gently to prevent them from browning. Thread the bananas, pineapple, orange, prunes and apricots onto the skewers, dividing the ingredients equally between them.

Put the orange juice, honey and mixed spice in a small bowl and mix. Brush over the fruit skewers. Cook the kebabs under a medium-hot grill for 5 minutes, turning frequently. Brush with any remaining orange juice mixture while they are cooking to prevent them from drying out. Serve warm, with some low-fat natural yoghurt.

variation: Use other fresh, tinned or dried fruits of your choice, such as pink grapefruit, peaches, kiwis, pears and large raisins. Use pineapple or apple juice in place of the orange juice. Use ground cinnamon or nutmeg instead of the mixed spice.

There are no limits to this breakfast indulgence, which can be made with any fruits you like. The top can be decorated as extravagantly as you dare using toasted desiccated coconut, flaked almonds or a purée of sieved raspberries dribbled over the top.

exotic fruit scrunch

crispy oat scrunch

75 g plain or brown flour

75 g whole rolled oats

50 g unsalted butter

50 g demerara sugar

cream topping

300 ml whipping cream

200 ml Greek yoghurt

35 g icing sugar or to taste

exotic fruit layers

2 medium papayas (about 500 g), peeled, deseeded and sliced

1 large mango (about 600 g), peeled, deseeded and sliced

2 fresh figs, quartered

4 passion fruit

a 30 x 20-cm baking sheet, greased

1 large glass serving bowl or 4 individual glasses

serves 4

Preheat the oven to 200°C (400°F) Gas 6.

To make the crispy oat scrunch, put the flour and oats in a medium bowl and mix well. Using your fingertips, rub in the butter until the mixture resembles breadcrumbs. Stir in the sugar, then press the mixture firmly onto the prepared sheet. Bake in the preheated oven for 15 minutes, or until lightly golden. Leave to cool, then break up into large random pieces.

To make the cream topping, whip the cream until soft peaks form. Stir in the yoghurt and add icing sugar, to taste.

Put the pieces of crispy oat scrunch in the bottom of 1 large serving bowl or 4 individual glasses, top with the papayas and mango, then the sweetened cream and yoghurt mixture. Finish with some passion fruit flesh and the figs.

After tasting this, you will forget all other granolas and feel virtuous knowing that you made your own. What's more, with such a delicious and nutritious breakfast inside you, you'll be set for the rest of the day. You can store the cereal in an airtight container for up to 4 weeks – if it lasts that long.

house granola

300 g rolled oats

50 g almonds

50 g raisins

25 g dried apricots

25 g pumpkin seeds

25 g golden caster sugar

4 tablespoons maple syrup

serves 4

Preheat the oven to 160°C (325°F) Gas 3.

Mix all the ingredients together in a large bowl, then transfer to a baking sheet. Bake in the preheated oven for 25 minutes, or until lightly toasted.

Remove from the oven and stir well. Return the mixture to the oven and cook for a further 15 minutes until the granola is crisp and light golden.

Remove from the oven. Serve hot or cold with milk.

What better way to start the day than with this soft muesli, steeped overnight in creamy yoghurt, then served topped with delicious summer berries and honey. Packed with goodness and a joy to eat before facing the day.

swiss muesli

200 g rolled oats

75 g bran flakes

75 g dried apple pieces

75 g raisins

75 g desiccated coconut

75 g chopped toasted hazelnuts

25 g sunflower seeds

450 ml natural yoghurt

to serve

500 g mixed fresh berries, such as blueberries, raspberries and strawberries

4 tablespoons honey

serves 4

Mix all the dry ingredients in a large bowl. Add the yoghurt, mix well, cover and chill overnight.

Serve in bowls with a scattering of berries and the honey drizzled over the top.

These recipes make a hearty breakfast that will keep you feeling full well up to lunchtime. And research shows that oats can help lower your cholesterol, so they're healthy, too. Both the Extra Oaty Porridge and All-in-one Oats are packed with essential vitamins, minerals and fibre.

extra oaty porridge

50 g jumbo porridge oats

1 tablespoon oatmeal

300 ml skimmed milk, plus extra to serve (optional)

25 g sultanas, chopped dates or chopped dried figs

1 banana, sliced

2 teaspoons honey or maple syrup

1 teaspoon flaked almonds

makes 1 large serving

Put the oats, oatmeal and milk in a large microwaveable bowl and mix well. Cover and microwave on high for 4 minutes, stirring halfway through.

Alternatively, you can put the oats, oatmeal and milk in a saucepan and cook over medium heat for 5 minutes, stirring continuously.

Transfer to a serving bowl, add the sultanas, banana and extra milk, if using. Spoon over the honey, sprinkle with the almonds and serve.

variation: Replace the almonds with finely chopped walnuts, hazelnuts or brazil nuts. Add slices of kiwi or peach instead of the banana, if you prefer.

all-in-one oats

base mixture

8 tablespoons oats

1 tablespoon chopped dried apricots

1 tablespoon sultanas

1 tablespoon finely chopped walnuts

1 tablespoon finely chopped almonds, brazil nuts or hazelnuts

to serve (per person)

½ apple, grated

150–300 ml skimmed milk

4 raspberries

4 blueberries

4 grapes

½ kiwi, sliced

1 tablespoon low-fat yoghurt (optional)

serves 4

Put the oats, dried apricots, sultanas and nuts in an airtight container, shake well and reserve. The night before you want to serve this for breakfast, pour about 3 tablespoons of the mixture into a large bowl. Add the grated apple and 150 ml milk. Stir well.

Cover and refrigerate overnight. Just before serving, add a little more skimmed milk to loosen the mixture, if you like. Add the raspberries, blueberries, grapes and kiwi. Serve topped with the low-fat yoghurt, if using.

These lovely chewy bars are made with a basic mixture of butter, honey, sugar, oats, flour and baking powder. You can add your own favourite dried fruits, seeds and nuts or you could replace the nuts with chopped dates, dried figs or dried cranberries.

muesli bars

100 g unsalted butter

130 g clear honey

2 tablespoons light brown muscovado sugar

300 g porridge oats

2 tablespoons plain flour

½ teaspoon baking powder

50 g dried apricots, chopped

2 tablespoons sunflower seeds

2 tablespoons sesame seeds

2 tablespoons raisins

100 g mixed nuts or dried fruit and nut mix, chopped

a 20.5 x 28-cm baking tin, lightly greased and base-lined

makes 16 bars

Preheat the oven to 160°C (325°F) Gas 3.

Put the butter, honey and sugar in a large saucepan over low heat. Heat gently until the butter melts, then remove from the heat. Stir gently with a wooden spoon. Tip the remaining ingredients into the pan and stir well.

Transfer the mixture to the prepared baking tin and spread evenly.

Bake for 30 minutes, or until golden brown. Remove the tin from the oven and put it on a wire rack. Leave to cool completely.

Run a round-bladed knife inside the edge of the tin, then invert onto a chopping board so the muesli mixture falls out in one piece. Cut into 16 bars. Store in an airtight container for up to 1 week.

sweet treats

This is the all-American classic, loved by millions for those lazy weekend mornings. You can use fresh or frozen berries, but frozen blueberries take slightly longer to cook and therefore don't burn so quickly.

blueberry soured cream pancakes
with maple syrup pecans

285 g plain flour

2 teaspoons baking powder

1 teaspoon salt

55 g caster sugar

2 eggs, separated

250 ml soured cream

150 ml milk

55 g unsalted butter, melted and cooled

250 g blueberries, fresh or frozen

vanilla ice cream, to serve

maple syrup pecans

100 g pecan halves

250 ml maple syrup

55 g unsalted butter

makes 8–10 pancakes

Preheat the oven to 200°C (400°F) Gas 6.

To make the maple syrup pecans, spread the pecan halves over a baking sheet and cook in the preheated oven for 5 minutes until lightly toasted. Simmer the maple syrup in a small saucepan for 3 minutes. Remove from the heat and stir in the pecans and butter.

To make the pancakes, sift the flour, baking powder, salt and sugar into a bowl. Put the egg yolks, soured cream, milk and butter into a second bowl and beat well, then add the flour mixture all at once and beat until smooth. Put the egg whites into a clean bowl and whisk until soft peaks form. Fold them gently into the batter, then fold in the blueberries. Do not overmix – a few lumps of flour and egg white don't matter.

Lightly grease a frying pan and preheat over medium heat. Reduce the heat. Pour 3 tablespoons of batter into the pan and cook in batches of 3–4 for 1–2 minutes over very low heat to avoid burning the blueberries, until small bubbles begin to appear on top and the underside is golden brown. Turn them over and cook the other side for 1 minute. Transfer to a plate and keep them warm in a low oven while you cook the remainder.

Serve with ice cream and the maple syrup pecans.

These pretty speckled pancakes are a treat. Orange zest gives the recipe a fresh edge while the poppyseeds provide a little crunch. Beware of the honey – too much and the pancakes will brown too quickly without giving the centre enough time to cook.

poppyseed pancakes
with spiced clementines

4 clementines or small oranges

150 g plain flour

½ teaspoon baking powder

½ teaspoon bicarbonate of soda

30 g soft brown sugar

50 g poppyseeds

1 egg

1 tablespoon honey

80 ml soured cream

80 ml milk

250 g mascarpone cheese, to serve

spiced brown sugar (makes 600 g)

400 g light muscovado sugar

200 g dark muscovado sugar

2 cinnamon sticks, broken,
plus 2 sticks to store

1 teaspoon allspice berries

1 teaspoon whole cloves

finely grated zest of
1 unwaxed lemon

makes 10–12 small pancakes

To make the spiced brown sugar, put both sugars in a food processor, add the broken cinnamon sticks, allspice, cloves and lemon zest and grind to a coarse powder. Sift through a wide-meshed sieve and discard any large pieces of spice. Store the spiced sugar in an airtight container with 2 cinnamon sticks.

To make the spiced clementines, grate the zest of 2 of the fruit, then peel all 4, removing as much of the bitter white pith as possible. Using a sharp knife, finely slice the fruit crossways. Arrange the fruit on a plate, sprinkle with 4 tablespoons of the spiced sugar and set aside to infuse.

To make the pancakes, sift the flour, baking powder and bicarbonate of soda in a large bowl, then stir in the brown sugar and poppyseeds.

Put the egg, honey, soured cream and milk into a second large bowl, then add the reserved grated zest of the clementines. Whisk well, then add the flour mixture all at once and keep whisking until just smooth.

Lightly grease a stove-top grill pan and warm over over medium heat. Reduce the heat. Pour 1 tablespoon of batter into the pan and cook in batches of 3–4 for 1 minute over low heat, until small bubbles begin to appear on the surface and the underside is golden brown. Turn the pancakes over and cook the other side for 1 minute. Transfer to a plate and keep them warm in a low oven while you cook the remainder.

To serve, layer the poppyseed pancakes with slices of clementines and spoonfuls of mascarpone.

Some mornings are made for indulgence. When complete chocolate overload is called for, make these pancakes. Packed with velvety melted chocolate and finished with the sweet-and-sour taste of smooth white chocolate yoghurt.

triple chocolate pancakes

285 g plain flour

75 g cocoa powder

1 teaspoon baking powder

1 teaspoon bicarbonate of soda

55 g caster sugar

200 ml milk

125 ml buttermilk

2 eggs, separated

30 g unsalted butter, melted and cooled

½ teaspoon salt

100 g dark chocolate, chopped

100 g white chocolate, chopped

ready-made chocolate sauce, to serve (optional)

white chocolate yoghurt

150 g white chocolate

4 tablespoons Greek yoghurt

makes about 12 pancakes

Sift the flour, cocoa, baking powder, bicarbonate of soda and sugar into a bowl. Put the milk, buttermilk, egg yolks and butter into a second large bowl and beat well. Add the flour mixture and mix thoroughly.

Put the egg whites and salt into a clean bowl and whisk until stiff peaks form. Add 1 tablespoon of the egg whites to the pancake mixture and stir to loosen it, then carefully fold in the remaining egg whites, then the dark and white chocolate.

Lightly grease a flat grill pan or frying pan and warm over medium heat. Reduce the heat. Pour about 2 tablespoons of batter into the pan and cook in batches of 3–4 over low heat for about 1 minute, or until small bubbles begin to appear on the surface and the underside is golden brown. Turn the pancakes over and cook the other side for 1 minute.

Transfer to a plate and keep them warm in a low oven while you cook the remainder. To make the white chocolate yoghurt, put the chocolate into a bowl set over a saucepan of simmering water and melt slowly. Remove from the heat and leave to cool a little, then beat in the yoghurt until the mixture is smooth and shiny. Serve with the pancakes and hot chocolate sauce, if using.

Adding sliced fruit to the top of any pancake turns it into something special and these apple-topped griddle cakes are no exception. Some fruits burn more quickly than others, so keep a close watch on the cakes while they are cooking.

date & pistachio griddle cakes

200 g plain flour

2 teaspoons baking powder

1 teaspoon salt

3 tablespoons light brown sugar

50 g rolled oats

100 g shelled, unsalted pistachio nuts, coarsely chopped

100 g dates, stoned and finely chopped

250 ml milk

2 eggs

55 g unsalted butter, melted and cooled, plus extra for brushing

grated zest of 1 lemon

2 apples

to serve

fresh honeycomb (optional)

Greek yoghurt or soured cream

makes 12 griddle cakes

Sift the flour, baking powder and salt into a large bowl, then stir in the sugar, oats, nuts and dates. Put the milk, eggs, butter and lemon zest into another bowl, beat well, then add the nut and oat mixture and stir gently. (Be careful not to overwork the mixture – it doesn't matter if the dough isn't smooth.)

Before you begin to cook the griddle cakes, prepare the apple by slicing it horizontally into 3-mm rings and removing the core of each slice with a pastry cutter (a star shape works best).

Lightly grease a flat griddle or frying pan over medium heat. Reduce the heat. Pour 1 tablespoon of batter onto the griddle and top with an apple slice. Cook in batches of 3–4 for 2–3 minutes over low heat, or until small bubbles begin to appear on the surface and the underside is golden brown. Brush the apple slice with a little melted butter, then turn the pancakes over and cook the other side for about 2 minutes. Repeat until all the mixture and apple slices have been used. Transfer to a plate and keep them warm in a low oven while you cook the remainder.

Serve immediately with honeycomb, if using, and Greek yoghurt.

This recipe has lovely autumnal associations. Allspice is the secret ingredient – it brings all the fruit and nut flavours together, and grinding your own allspice berries – in a dedicated pepper grinder – will make sure you get the full force of the spice.

apple wholemeal waffles
with sugar plums

225 g plain flour

75 g wholemeal flour

2 teaspoons baking powder

½ teaspoon salt

2 tablespoons soft dark brown sugar

1 teaspoon ground allspice

50 g pecan nuts, chopped

2 eggs, separated

200 ml milk

1 tablespoon molasses

55 g unsalted butter,
melted and cooled

2 crisp apples, peeled, cored
and coarsely chopped

sugar plums

6 ripe plums, quartered and stoned

110 g spiced brown sugar (page 41)

30 g unsalted butter

freshly squeezed juice of ½ lemon

a deep Belgian waffle iron

makes 8 deep Belgian-sized waffles

To make the sugar plums, put the quartered plums and spiced brown sugar into a bowl and toss to coat. Melt the butter in a small frying pan over medium heat until it foams, then add all the plum pieces and gently sauté until caramelized. Add the lemon juice to loosen the butter syrup and set aside to keep warm while you prepare the waffles.

Lightly grease the waffle iron and preheat.

To make the waffles, put the plain and wholemeal flours into a large bowl, add the baking powder, salt, sugar, allspice and pecan nuts and stir well.

Put the egg yolks into another bowl, add the milk, molasses and butter and beat well. Add the flour mixture, stir well, then stir in the chopped apple. Put the egg whites into a clean, grease-free bowl and whisk until stiff peaks form, then fold gently into the waffle batter with a metal spoon.

Spoon about 125 ml of the batter into the preheated waffle iron compartments, making sure each batch has lots of apple in it. Adjust the amount of batter according to the size of your iron. Cook until crisp, about 3–5 minutes. The waffles should be crisp on the outside and served immediately. At a pinch, they can be kept warm in a low oven, but will lose some crispness. A quick reheating in the toaster works remarkably well.

Serve the waffles immediately, topped with warm plums and plenty of sticky plum juice.

Belgian waffles are traditionally thick, with deep wells to trap butter and syrup. The best use a yeast-raised batter and it's definitely worth the effort. By doing the hard work the night before, all you need to do in the morning is add the eggs and bake.

classic belgian waffles
with strawberries & praline cream

285 g plain flour

2 tablespoons caster sugar

1 teaspoon salt

1 teaspoon easy-blend dried yeast

140 g unsalted butter,
melted and cooled

375 ml milk

1 teaspoon vanilla extract

3 eggs, separated

250 g strawberries, to serve

praline cream

300 ml double cream

55 g shop-bought hazelnut brittle,
ground to a powder in a spice grinder

a deep Belgian waffle iron

makes 12 waffles

Start the night before. Sift the flour, sugar, salt and yeast into a large bowl. Stir in the butter, milk and vanilla extract to make a smooth mixture. Cover the bowl with clingfilm and leave at room temperature overnight.

First thing in the morning, lightly grease the waffle iron and preheat. Beat the egg yolks into the yeast mixture. Put the egg whites into a clean, grease-free bowl and whisk until stiff peaks form. Carefully fold them into the batter with a metal spoon.

To make the praline cream, put the cream into a clean bowl and whip to a soft, loose consistency. Stir in the ground hazelnut brittle.

Pour about 125 ml of batter into the preheated waffle iron compartments. Adjust the amount of batter according to the size of your iron. Cook until golden, about 3–5 minutes. The waffles should be crisp on the outside and served immediately. At a pinch, they can be kept warm in a low oven, but will lose some crispness. A quick reheating in the toaster works remarkably well.

Serve the waffles hot with a spoonful of the praline cream and a few fresh strawberries.

These delicate waffles are jam-packed with fruit. As the batter cooks, the raspberries soften and the juice seeps into the fabric of the waffle giving a beautiful red mottled effect. Soured cream on the side will counteract the delicious sweetness of the honey.

raspberry waffles
with peach & pistachio honey

285 g plain flour

2 teaspoons baking powder

½ teaspoon salt

3 tablespoons caster sugar

3 eggs, separated

225 ml milk

55 g unsalted butter, melted and cooled

2 teaspoons vanilla extract

150 g fresh raspberries

soured cream, to serve (optional)

peach & pistachio honey

2 firm peaches, skinned and stoned

350 ml clear orange-blossom honey

1 tablespoon peach schnapps (optional)

50 g shelled unsalted pistachios

a waffle iron

makes 8 waffles

To make the peach and pistachio honey, cut the peaches into 3-mm cubes. Put the honey and schnapps, if using, in a saucepan and heat until almost boiling. Remove the pan from the heat, add the chopped peaches and the pistachios and leave to cool slightly.

Lightly grease the waffle iron and preheat.

To make the waffles, sift the flour, baking powder, salt and sugar in a large bowl. Put the egg yolks, milk, butter and vanilla extract in a separate bowl and beat well. Add the dry ingredients to the egg mixture and stir until just mixed. Add the raspberries to the batter, crushing some with the back of a spoon to give a marbled effect.

Put the egg whites in a clean, grease-free bowl and whisk until stiff peaks form. Gently fold them into the waffle batter using a large metal spoon.

Spoon 4–8 tablespoons of batter into each preheated compartment. Adjust the amount of batter according to the size of your iron. Cook until golden, about 4–5 minutes. The waffles should be crisp on the outside and served immediately. At a pinch, they can be kept warm in a low oven, but will lose some crispness. A quick reheating in the toaster works remarkably well.

Serve the waffles warm, topped with a spoonful of the peach and pistachio honey and some soured cream, if using.

Doughnuts have long made a quick and substantial fresh breakfast and this remains true today, especially in America. This is based on an old Irish settler recipe and uses mashed floury potatoes for speed and flavour. The spices make it an absolute winner.

breakfast doughnuts

450 g plain flour

¼ teaspoon sea salt

½ teaspoon ground ginger

½ teaspoon ground cinnamon

½ teaspoon freshly grated nutmeg

1½ teaspoons bicarbonate of soda

200 g golden caster sugar

40 g unsalted butter, diced

225 g very smooth mashed potatoes

2 eggs, beaten

230 ml buttermilk (or a mixture of half natural yoghurt and half semi-skimmed milk)

vegetable oil, for deep-frying

cinnamon sugar

2 tablespoons caster sugar

1 teaspoon ground cinnamon

a deep-fat fryer

makes 12 doughnuts

Mix the flour with the salt, spices, bicarbonate of soda and sugar in a large bowl. Rub in the butter with the tips of your fingers until the mixture resembles breadcrumbs.

Add the mashed potatoes, mix briefly, then add the eggs and enough of the buttermilk to make a soft dough. If the dough feels very sticky, add extra flour 1 tablespoon at a time.

Turn out the dough onto a lightly floured work surface and knead for a few seconds until it is just smooth. Roll it out 1.5 cm thick, then cut out rounds using an 8-cm round biscuit cutter (or upturned glass). Stamp out the centre of each round with a 2-cm round biscuit cutter. Re-roll the trimmings and centre circles, then cut out more rings.

Fill a deep-fat fryer with vegetable oil to the manufacturer's recommended level. Heat the oil to 180°C (350°F), or until a cube of bread browns in about 40 seconds. Fry the doughnuts 2 or 3 at a time, turning them frequently until well browned and cooked through, about 4 minutes. Remove from the oil with a slotted spoon and drain well on kitchen paper.

Mix the cinnamon sugar ingredients together, sprinkle over the doughnuts, then serve warm with coffee. They are best eaten within 24 hours.

Dream of Seville, Madrid and Barcelona when you eat these doughnuts. Serve with hot chocolate and it will complete the illusion. It is essential to cook the extruded batter in very hot olive oil, to crisp and seal the outside and steam the batter inside.

churros
with hot chocolate

350 g self-raising flour

½ teaspoon salt

1 egg, beaten

400–450 ml milk

light olive oil, for deep-frying

8 tablespoons caster sugar

4 tablespoons ground cinnamon (optional)

hot chocolate

250 g bitter dark chocolate, chopped or grated

600 ml milk, boiled

a piping bag fitted with a 1–2 cm plain nozzle

serves 4

Sift the flour and salt in a bowl and make a well in the centre. Whisk the egg in a bowl with 250 ml of the milk. Pour into the well and whisk into the flour. Gradually whisk in enough of the remaining milk to make a smooth, creamy, thick batter able to be piped easily. Transfer to the prepared piping bag.

Pour a 10-cm depth of olive oil into a heavy-based saucepan fitted with a frying basket. Heat the oil to 190°C (375°F), or until a cube of bread browns in 35 seconds.

Pipe long, spiralled, coiled-up lengths of batter directly into the oil. Leave to sizzle and cook for 4–6 minutes, or until golden and spongy in the centre (test one to check).

Lift the churros out of the oil using the basket or tongs. Drain on crumpled kitchen paper. Repeat using the remaining doughnut mixture.

When cool, scissor-snip the churros into 15-cm lengths. Put the caster sugar in a plate, mix in the cinnamon, if using, then roll the pieces in the mixture.

To make the hot chocolate, mix the chocolate and boiled milk together in a small saucepan, whisking and cooking until the chocolate is well blended and the liquid is dusky brown. Serve in 4 cups or bowls with the churros.

These corn cakes are eaten at street fairs, bars and markets all over Colombia and Venezuela. Arepa meal (*masarepa*), sold in delicatessens or Hispanic markets, is a ready-cooked flour made from very starchy cooked corn.

arepas
yellow corn cakes with fruit batidas

250 g fresh or frozen sweetcorn kernels

250 g yellow arepa meal (*masarepa*) or semolina

125 g cheese, such as Mexican *queso fresco* or mozzarella, grated

125 g Cheddar cheese, grated

1 teaspoon baking powder

½ teaspoon salt

40 g caster sugar

2 fresh serrano or jalapeño chillies, deseeded and chopped

60 ml milk

corn oil, for brushing

fresh fruit batida

assorted tropical fruit, such as mango, guava, melon and papaya

sugar syrup, to taste

makes 18 arepas

To make the fresh fruit batida, peel and stone (where necessary) your choice of tropical fruit. Put through a juicer or purée in a blender. Add sugar syrup to taste, plus crushed ice and mineral water if necessary.

To make the arepas, grind the corn kernels in a food processor until fine. Transfer to a bowl, then mix in the arepa meal, the cheeses, baking powder, salt, sugar and chillies. Mix the milk with 1 tablespoon hot water, stir into the flour mixture and mix to a stiff dough. Divide into 18 portions, roll into balls and flatten into patties about 1 cm thick.

Preheat a stove-top grill pan or frying pan, brush with oil, add the arepas, in batches and cook over low to medium heat for 3 minutes on each side, until golden and crusty outside and soft inside.

Serve with the fresh fruit batida and a cup of strong black coffee.

For many of us, French toast conjures up comforting memories of childhood. Why not recreate that nostalgia next time you have a few minutes to spare on a weekend morning? The most important thing is to use top-quality ingredients – the best white bread (or even brioche), the creamiest unsalted butter and finest ground cinnamon.

french toast

4 slices thick-cut white bread, brioche or challah

2 large eggs, beaten

2 tablespoons single cream

½ teaspoon vanilla extract

3½ tablespoons golden caster sugar

about 50 g unsalted butter, for frying

½ teaspoon ground cinnamon

maple syrup, to serve (optional)

serves 4

Trim the crusts from the bread, then cut the slices in half. Put the eggs, cream, vanilla extract and 1 teaspoon of the sugar in a shallow dish and mix with a fork.

Heat half the butter in a large, heavy, non-stick frying pan. When the butter is foaming, thoroughly coat a piece of bread in the egg mixture, drain off the excess and put it in the hot butter. Add 3 more pieces of coated bread to the pan in the same way, then cook over medium heat for 3–4 minutes until the underside is golden brown. Turn over and cook the other side. Meanwhile, mix the remaining sugar and cinnamon in a small sugar shaker or bowl. Put the cooked bread on a warm serving plate and sprinkle with some of the cinnamon sugar.

Wipe out the frying pan, reheat and cook the remaining pieces of bread as before. Serve hot, sprinkled with more cinnamon sugar and maple syrup, if using.

variation: To make cinnamon toast, heat the grill, toast thick slices of bread on both sides, then butter thoroughly. Mix the cinnamon sugar as in the above recipe, and sprinkle generously to cover. Put the toast back under the grill until the sugar starts to melt and bubble. Remove carefully and eat when the toast has cooled enough not to burn your lips (the top will look like a brandy snap – lacy and crisp).

Somewhere between a light and fluffy bread-and-butter pudding and an unbelievably squidgy French toast, this is a divine concoction. Panettone is a sweet yeast bread traditionally eaten at Christmas in Italy.

creamy orange french toast

60 ml single cream

2 large egg yolks

freshly grated zest of
½ unwaxed orange

2 teaspoons freshly squeezed orange juice

1 teaspoon sugar

15 g unsalted butter

2 thick slices of panettone, cut in half

icing sugar, to dust

strips of orange zest, to decorate

orange cream

3 tablespoons crème fraîche

1 teaspoon icing sugar

1 tablespoon orange juice

½ teaspoon lemon juice

serves 2

To make the orange cream, put the crème fraîche, icing sugar, orange juice and lemon juice in a bowl and stir until smooth and creamy. Set aside.

Put the cream, egg yolks, grated orange zest and juice and the sugar in a wide, shallow dish and beat well. Heat the butter in a large, non-stick frying pan. Dip each slice of panettone in the custard mixture, coating each side well, then arrange in the pan. Spoon any remaining custard mixture over the toasts and fry for 2 minutes, or until golden underneath.

Very carefully flip the toasts over and cook for a further 1–2 minutes until golden. Put 2 slices of French toast on each plate, then dust with icing sugar, drizzle over the orange cream and top with strips of orange zest.

Using coconut milk instead of regular milk and Italian panettone instead of bread adds a mouth-watering twist to this simple breakfast dish. For a slightly healthier version, you can serve it with yoghurt instead of cream.

panettone french toast
with coconut milk

½ **vanilla pod**

150 ml tinned coconut milk

2 eggs, lightly beaten

25 g caster sugar

¼ **teaspoon ground cardamom (optional)**

50 g unsalted butter

8 slices of panettone or other sweet bread

to serve

icing sugar, to dust

blueberries

clotted or whipped cream

serves 4

Split the vanilla pod in half lengthways and scrape out the seeds. Put the coconut milk, eggs, sugar, vanilla seeds and cardamom, if using, in a bowl and beat well. Pour the mixture into a shallow dish.

Heat half the butter in a large frying pan. Dip 2 slices of panettone into the egg mixture and sauté until golden on both sides, about 2 minutes for each side. Repeat with the remaining slices and serve dusted with icing sugar and topped with the blueberries and cream.

This luscious toast falls somewhere between a free-form summer pudding and an indulgent trifle, with the sweet, alcoholic juices soaking into the brioche and the rich, creamy mascarpone sliding off the top. You can use any combination of summer berries, but I like strawberries and blueberries the best.

macerated berries
on brioche french toast

100 g strawberries, hulled

50 g blueberries

1 teaspoon sugar

2½ tablespoons Grand Marnier

80 ml mascarpone cheese

1 tablespoon icing sugar

2 thick slices of brioche

fresh mint leaves, to serve (optional)

serves 2

Halve or quarter the strawberries, depending on size, and put in a bowl with the blueberries. Sprinkle with the sugar, then add the Grand Marnier and leave to macerate for at least 1 hour.

Just before serving, put the mascarpone and icing sugar in a bowl and stir in 2–3 teaspoons of the macerating juices from the berries.

Lightly toast the brioche on both sides, then spread with a thick layer of mascarpone and spoon the macerated berries and all the juices on top. Top with fresh mint leaves, if using, and serve.

Quince paste is available from specialist shops and delicatessens, and is worth seeking out for its distinctive flavour. As an alternative, you can also use raspberry preserve or redcurrant jelly.

sweet bruschetta
with quince-glazed figs

2 tablespoons quince paste

25 g butter

2 tablespoons port

12 ripe figs, halved

4 slices of brioche or challah

icing sugar and cinnamon, to dust

Greek yoghurt, to serve

serves 4

Put the quince paste, butter and port in a saucepan and heat gently until melted. Arrange the figs, cut-side up, in an ovenproof dish. Spoon over the port mixture, making sure the surface of each fig is well covered.

Put under a hot grill and cook for 3–5 minutes, until the figs are caramelized and heated through.

Meanwhile, toast the brioche on a stove-top grill pan. Transfer to warmed serving plates and sprinkle with icing sugar and cinnamon. Top with the figs and serve with Greek yoghurt.

This is the ultimate in no-fuss indulgence. For best results, choose a really good lemon curd and a thick, mild-tasting yoghurt. Check the flavour of the lemon cream once you've mixed it up – if you use a bland lemon curd, you may have to add a little extra.

toasted brioche
with lemon cream & fresh raspberries

100 ml crème fraîche

100 ml natural yoghurt

3–4 tablespoons lemon curd

3–4 individual brioche buns or
6–8 thick slices of brioche

about 150 g fresh raspberries

icing sugar, to dust (optional)

serves 3–4

Put the crème fraîche, yoghurt and lemon curd in a bowl and mix briefly. Set aside.

Cut the brioche buns in half and lightly toast under a hot grill. Arrange the base of each brioche on a plate, spoon the lemon cream mixture on top, then pile on the raspberries. Add the toasted lid, dust with icing sugar, if using, and serve immediately.

big bites

Cheese on toast has always been a popular comfort food, so what better way start your weekend than with an oozing cheese waffle on which to build your favourite brunch. Most cheeses – from cottage cheese to Cheddar to Parmesan – will work.

morning-after
breakfast waffles

180 g plain flour

120 g fine cornmeal

2 teaspoons baking powder

½ teaspoon sea salt

2 eggs, separated

225 ml milk

200 ml soured cream or yoghurt

2 tablespoons olive oil, plus extra for frying and roasting

120 g Cheddar cheese, grated

2 tablespoons snipped fresh chives

to serve

20 cherry tomatoes on the vine

16 bacon rashers

8 eggs

sea salt and freshly ground black pepper

a waffle iron

makes 8 waffles

Preheat the oven to 200°C (400°F) Gas 6 and grease a baking sheet. Lightly grease and preheat the waffle iron.

Put the vine tomatoes on the prepared baking sheet, sprinkle with olive oil, season and roast for 5 minutes or until their skins blister.

To make the waffles, sift the flour, cornmeal, baking powder and salt in a large bowl. Put the egg yolks into another bowl, add the milk, soured cream and olive oil and whisk well. Add the flour mixture and beat well. Put the egg whites in a clean bowl and whisk until stiff peaks form. Using a large metal spoon, gently fold the egg whites, Cheddar and chives into the waffle batter.

Brush a small frying pan with olive oil and heat well. Add the bacon and fry until crisp. Remove from the pan and leave to drain on kitchen paper. Brush the pan with oil again, add 4 rashers of the cooked bacon, then break 2 eggs on top and fry gently until the eggs are cooked. Set aside to keep warm.

Spoon 125 ml of the batter into the preheated waffle iron compartments. Adjust the amount of batter according to the size of your iron. Cook until crisp, at least 4–5 minutes (cheese waffles taste so much better when well done). Transfer to a large plate, slide the bacon and eggs on top and serve with the roasted tomatoes. Repeat to make the other servings.

This dish makes a good breakfast when you're feeling a little the worse for wear – it is great comfort food and is sure to fill you up. Choose a good floury potato, such as desirée, to ensure the perfect texture for the hash browns.

hash browns
with sausages & oven-roasted tomatoes

750 g floury potatoes, diced

50 g butter

1 large onion, finely chopped

12 good-quality sausages

2 tablespoons olive oil

500 g cherry tomatoes on the vine

1 tablespoon balsamic vinegar

sea salt and freshly ground
black pepper

serves 4

Preheat the oven to 200°C (400°F) Gas 6. Lightly grease a baking sheet.

Cook the potatoes in a large saucepan of lightly salted boiling water for 10–12 minutes, until almost cooked through. Drain and mash roughly.

Melt the butter in a large, non-stick frying pan and gently fry the onion for 15 minutes, until soft and golden. Add the potatoes and seasoning. Cook, stirring and mashing the potatoes occasionally, for about 15–20 minutes, or until well browned and crispy around the edges.

Meanwhile, put the sausages in a roasting tin, drizzle with half the oil and roast on the middle shelf of the oven for 25 minutes.

Once the sausages are in the oven, put the vine tomatoes on the prepared baking sheet. Drizzle with the remaining oil and put on the top shelf of the oven after the sausages have been cooking for 5 minutes. Cook for about 15 minutes, then drizzle over the balsamic vinegar and cook for a further 5 minutes.

Spoon the hash browns onto plates and top with the sausages, tomatoes and their juices.

Great for breakfast, but just as good for brunch, lunch, a mid-afternoon snack or midnight feast, this winning combination of toasted croissant, melting Gruyère, wafer-thin slices of ham and juicy fresh peaches can't be beaten. It's good made with wedges of fresh fig too.

melting cheese & ham croissants

1 teaspoon wholegrain mustard

1 teaspoon balsamic vinegar

1 tablespoon olive oil

2 slices of prosciutto or other wafer-thin cured ham, about 25 g

½ ripe peach

2 croissants

2 large slices of Swiss cheese, such as Gruyère or Emmental, about 60 g

serves 2

Preheat the grill to hot.

Put the mustard, vinegar and oil in a bowl, mix well, then set aside. Cut the ham slices in half lengthways to make 4 long strips. Slice the peach into thin wedges.

Split the croissants in half and arrange on a grill tray, cut-side down. Cook under the preheated grill for about 2 minutes until very lightly toasted, then flip over and fold a slice of cheese on the bottom half of each one. Grill until the cheese is melting, and the top halves are golden. (The top halves will be done just before the cheese-covered halves, so remove and keep them warm.)

Arrange the ham and peach wedges over the melting cheese, drizzle over the dressing, top with the second half of the croissant and serve.

When you require both style and substance first thing, make these breakfast kebabs. Visually impressive thanks to the tomatoes, peppers and onions, and protein-packed, you'll be set up for the day. The onion can be replaced with a large, flat field mushroom.

breakfast kebabs

½ **red pepper**

½ **green pepper**

½ **yellow pepper**

4 **back bacon rashers**

1 **small red onion**

8 **cherry tomatoes or baby plum tomatoes**

8 **small cocktail sausages**

4 **soft wholemeal rolls or pita breads**

4 wooden skewers, soaked in warm water for 10 minutes

makes 4 kebabs

Preheat the oven to 220°C (425°F) Gas 7 and grease a large roasting tin.

Deseed the peppers then cut them into large chunks. Cut each rasher of bacon in half, then roll up. Cut the onion into quarters. Leave the tomatoes and sausages whole.

Thread the peppers, bacon, onion, tomatoes and sausages onto the wooden skewers, leaving a small gap between each piece on the skewer. Put them in any order you like, but make sure each skewer has an equal amount of each ingredient.

Arrange the kebabs in the prepared roasting tin, slightly apart. Bake for 15–20 minutes, or until golden. Meanwhile, warm the bread rolls, either in the toaster or in a second oven on a low temperature. Put a kebab on each serving plate and serve immediately with the warmed bread.

You can keep any of this lovely leftover garlic mayonnaise covered and refrigerated for up to three days. Both it and the shallot jam are very good served with many other dishes. Try the jam with sausages, and the mayonnaise with chips or baked potatoes.

mushroom burgers
with shallot jam & garlic mayonnaise

4 large portobello mushrooms

1 tablespoon extra virgin olive oil

4 large ciabatta rolls

sea salt and freshly ground
black pepper

mixed salad, to serve

shallot jam

1 tablespoon extra virgin olive oil

125 g shallots, thinly sliced

2 tablespoons redcurrant jelly

1 tablespoon red wine vinegar

garlic mayonnaise

1 egg yolk

1 garlic clove, peeled and crushed

1 teaspoon freshly squeezed
lemon juice

a pinch of sea salt

150 ml light olive oil

serves 4

To make the shallot jam, heat the olive oil in a small frying pan and cook the shallots for 15 minutes. Add 1 tablespoon water, the redcurrant jelly and the vinegar. Cook for a further 10–15 minutes, or until reduced and thickened. Season to taste and leave to cool.

To make the mayonnaise, put the egg yolk, garlic, lemon juice and salt in a bowl and whisk until blended. Gradually whisk in the olive oil, a little at a time, until thickened and glossy.

Trim the mushrooms, brush all over with the olive oil and sprinkle with seasoning. Add to a hot non-stick frying pan and cook for 4–5 minutes each side. Cut the ciabatta rolls in half and toast on a preheated stove-top grill pan. Put the mushrooms on 4 of the toasted ciabatta halves and top with shallot jam, mayonnaise and the remaining ciabatta halves. Serve with mixed salad.

There's nothing quite like a warm sausage-filled roll for brunch. Dotting the sausages with mustard and wrapping them in bacon just adds to the taste experience and the cooking smells will waken even the most hung-over.

sausage & bacon rolls

a little mustard (any kind)

16 thin slices of Italian pancetta or streaky bacon

8 good-quality sausages

olive oil, for brushing

to serve

4 warm buttered soft rolls or even small naan bread or pita bread

tomato ketchup or grilled tomatoes

serves 4

Preheat the grill to medium.

Spread a little mustard over each slice of bacon. Wrap 2 slices around each sausage. Put the sausages on the rack of a grilling pan so that the loose ends of the bacon are underneath the sausages.

Brush with a little olive oil. Cook under the grill for about 6–8 minutes on each side, depending on the thickness of the sausage, or until the bacon is crisp and the sausage cooked through. Serve in buttered rolls with plenty of ketchup or grilled tomatoes.

Blini – little Russian pancakes – are usually made with buckwheat flour, topped with soured cream and caviar or smoked salmon. They are equally good made with mashed potato: the result is light and particularly delicious with salty salmon and crème fraîche.

fluffy potato pancakes
with smoked salmon

500 g floury potatoes

150 ml crème fraîche or double cream

3 eggs, separated

4 tablespoons snipped fresh chives

4 tablespoons unsalted butter

sea salt and freshly ground
black pepper

to serve

500 g sliced smoked salmon

300 ml crème fraîche

1 small bunch of chives, chopped

*4 blini pans or a non-stick frying pan
and 4 ring moulds*

serves 4

Boil the potatoes until tender, then drain. Mash, then beat in the cream and egg yolks. Season and beat in the chives.

Whisk the egg whites in a clean, grease-free bowl until stiff but not dry and fold into the potatoes.

Heat 4 blini pans, or a non-stick frying pan and 4 ring moulds. Add ½ tablespoon butter to each blini pan or 2 tablespoons to the frying pan. When the butter is foaming, spoon in about 4 tablespoons of the mixture into each pan or ring mould. Cook until browning and set, then flip over and cook for 1 minute more. Remove from the pans to a tea cloth and keep warm in the cloth. Repeat with the remaining butter and potato mixture.

Serve the potato pancakes topped with crinkled smoked salmon, a dollop of crème fraîche and some snipped chives.

Masa harina and chilli give this recipe a slightly Mexican flavour. If you wish to continue this theme, try these pancakes with huevos rancheros or even avocado salsa. Otherwise, serve with fried portobello mushrooms, cherry tomatoes and eggs.

cornmeal & bacon breakfast stack

100 g plain flour

1½ teaspoons baking powder

60 g *masa harina* or fine cornmeal

1 egg, separated

100 ml buttermilk

200 ml milk

2 tablespoons freshly grated Parmesan cheese

150 g streaky bacon, chopped

4 spring onions, cut into 1-cm slices

1 medium green chilli, deseeded and thinly sliced

sea salt and freshly ground black pepper

4 ring moulds, 9 cm diameter, greased

makes 4 pancakes

Preheat the oven to 200°C (400°F) Gas 6. Lightly grease a flat grill pan or large frying pan and warm over medium heat.

Sift the flour, baking powder and 1 teaspoon salt in a large bowl, then stir in the *masa harina*. Put the egg yolks in another bowl, add the buttermilk and milk and beat well. Add the flour mixture and beat to a thick batter. Stir in the Parmesan. Put the egg white into a clean, grease-free bowl and whisk until stiff peaks form, then fold into the batter using a metal spoon.

Add the prepared muffin rings to the grill pan or frying pan and heat well. Divide the bacon between the 4 muffin rings and fry for 1 minute. Add a share of the spring onions and chilli, then add 2 tablespoons of the batter to each ring. When the mixture has risen and started to set, remove the rings. Turn the pancakes over and cook until brown. Transfer to a plate and keep them warm in a low oven until you're ready to serve.

Rösti are a Swiss classic. These soft buttery pancakes are usually topped with wild mushrooms but can also be served topped with fried eggs, sprinkled with Gruyère cheese or served separately with meat and sausages.

swiss rösti

1 kg potatoes, unpeeled and well scrubbed

175 g clarified butter*

1 onion, chopped

125 g pancetta or streaky bacon, cut into thin strips

500 g wild or flat field mushrooms, or a mixture of both, cut in halves or quarters if large

2 tablespoons chopped fresh flat leaf parsley

sea salt and freshly ground black pepper

serves 4

*To clarify butter, melt over gentle heat, then leave to cool. Skim off the pure butter and discard the solids and water.

Put the potatoes in a large pan and cover with cold water. Bring to the boil and cook for 10–15 minutes, or until just tender. Drain well and leave to cool slightly. Peel, then grate coarsely into a large bowl.

Heat 2 tablespoons of the butter in a frying pan, add the onion and bacon and cook for 5–6 minutes, or until the onions are softened. Tip this mixture into the bowl of potato, season and mix well.

Heat half the remaining butter in a pan, add the potato mixture and press down slightly to form a large pancake. Cook for 10 minutes, adding a little extra butter around the edges and shaking the pan occasionally.

Carefully cover the pan with a large plate and flip over. Add more butter, then slide the rösti back in to cook the other side. Add butter around the edge and cook until golden, about 7 minutes. Remove from the heat and keep warm.

Heat the remaining butter in a frying pan. Add the mushrooms and cook, stirring occasionally, for 3–5 minutes, or until tender but still firm. Season and stir in the chopped parsley. Serve the rösti with the mushrooms.

Almost everyone loves a bacon sandwich and this is a really healthy, quick and easy version. The combination of hot tomato, fresh basil and sizzling bacon makes a fabulous taste-sensation that is perfect for breakfast or brunch.

bacon, tomato & basil toasty

2 extra-lean bacon rashers

1 tomato, sliced

1 thick slice of stoneground wholemeal or wholegrain bread

2 teaspoons chopped fresh basil

sea salt and freshly ground black pepper

serves 1

Put the bacon slices on a grill tray and cook under a preheated hot grill for 2 minutes. Add the tomato slices to the tray and cook for a further 2 minutes. Turn the bacon over and add the slice of bread to the tray. Let the bread go golden brown on one side before turning over and lightly toasting the other side.

Remove the grill tray from the heat. Put the bacon on the lightly toasted side of the bread, top with the tomato slices and basil, then season to taste. Return the grill tray to the heat and cook for a further 2 minutes. Serve immediately.

variation: For a more substantial snack, rub the bread with a halved garlic clove before toasting. Cut the garlic clove into thin slivers and insert into the tomato slices, then grill. Put the tomatoes on top of the bread, sprinkle with some Parmesan cheese shavings and serve with a green salad.

If you're a fan of baked beans, you should really try making your own – you'll be thrilled with the result. Traditionally, dried beans would have been used in this dish (often called Boston baked beans) but using tinned reduces the cooking time by two-thirds.

homemade baked beans

1 small gammon knuckle

800 g tinned borlotti beans, drained and rinsed

1 garlic clove, peeled and crushed

1 onion, finely chopped

450 ml vegetable stock

300 ml passata

2 tablespoons molasses or black treacle

2 tablespoons tomato purée

1 tablespoon soft dark brown sugar

1 tablespoon Dijon mustard

1 tablespoon red wine vinegar

freshly ground black pepper

freshly made toast, to serve

a large, flameproof casserole

serves 6

Soak the gammon overnight in cold water.

The next day, preheat the oven to 170°C (325°F) Gas 3.

Drain the gammon, wash and pat dry with kitchen paper. Put into a large, flameproof casserole.

Add the beans and all the remaining ingredients to the casserole. Cover and bring slowly to the boil on top of the stove, then transfer to the preheated oven and bake for 1½ hours. Remove the lid and cook for a further 30–45 minutes, until the sauce is syrupy.

Remove the gammon to a board and slice the meat. Put the toast onto serving plates, top with the beans and gammon and serve hot.

These noodles are not long and thin as one might think, but rather little fried squares of potato and semolina served either savoury or sweet. This sweet cherry compote is based on an original German recipe.

potato noodles
with red cherry compote

500 g floury potatoes, unpeeled

600 ml milk

75 g fine semolina

2 eggs, beaten

75 g caster sugar

½ teaspoon ground cinnamon

75 g butter

soured cream, to serve

50 g flaked almonds, toasted, to scatter

red cherry compote

500 g sweet red cherries, stoned

25 g caster sugar

1 strip of unwaxed orange zest

freshly squeezed juice of 1 orange

2 tablespoons Kirsch

a 33 x 22 x 1.5-cm Swiss roll tin, lightly greased

serves 4

Put the potatoes in a saucepan, cover with cold water, bring to the boil, then simmer for 25–30 minutes until tender. When cool enough to handle, peel and pass through a potato ricer into a clean saucepan.

Put the saucepan on the heat and gradually whisk in the milk until smooth. Cook, whisking continuously (do not allow to catch or burn) until it starts to boil. Sprinkle in the semolina in a thin stream, whisking all the time. Continue cooking until the mixture thickens. Remove from the heat and beat in the eggs. Spread onto the prepared Swiss roll tin, smoothing the surface. Leave to cool completely.

Turn the mixture out onto a work surface and cut into 2.5-cm strips. Cut across again into small squares or diamonds.

To make the red cherry compote, put the cherries in a saucepan with the sugar, orange zest and juice. Stir well, bring to the boil, reduce the heat, cover and simmer for 5–10 minutes or until the cherries are tender. Remove from the heat and stir in the Kirsch. Set aside.

Put the sugar and cinnamon in a pan, heat well and stir, then transfer to a large plate or tray.

Melt the butter in a large frying pan and cook the potato squares until lightly golden on both sides. Drain well on kitchen paper then transfer them to the tray of cinnamon sugar and toss well to coat, shaking off any excess.

Serve with soured cream and the warm compote, scattered with the toasted almonds.

You can't mess about with a classic like this because the old way is still the best. All you need is warm, squidgy bagels toasted until just crisp, then slathered with creamy cheese, layers of smoked salmon and a good squeeze of lemon juice.

toasted bagels
with cream cheese & smoked salmon

2 bagels

100 g cream cheese

125 g smoked salmon slices

lemon wedges, for squeezing

freshly ground black pepper

serves 2

Split the bagels in half horizontally and toast on both sides in a toaster, under the grill or using a stove-top grill pan.

Spread the bottom half of each bagel with cream cheese and fold the slices of smoked salmon on top. Squeeze over plenty of lemon juice, sprinkle with black pepper and serve topped with the second half of the bagel.

'Welsh rabbit' – also known as rarebit – is a glorified version of cheese on toast. It dates back to the mid-sixteenth century and has evolved into countless variations. This easy-to-make rarebit is hard to beat as a comforting snack or light brunch.

rarebit

25 g butter

4 shallots or 1 onion, sliced

100 g Cheddar or Gruyère cheese, grated

75 ml ale or lager

1 teaspoon mustard

a pinch of sea salt

2 eggs, lightly beaten

4 slices of bread

freshly ground black pepper

serves 2–4

Melt the butter in a heavy-based saucepan, add the shallots and cook until softened. Add the cheese, ale, mustard and salt. Stir over low heat until the cheese has melted.

Add the beaten eggs and stir until the mixture has thickened slightly, about 2–3 minutes. Don't overcook it or you will end up with scrambled eggs.

Meanwhile, toast the bread on both sides, then spoon the cheese mixture onto the toast and cook under a hot grill until puffed and gold-flecked. Serve with lots of black pepper.

We all get the munchies, especially if we've missed breakfast. Instead of reaching for that packet of crisps or bar of chocolate, make one of these snacks for brunch. Pure, fresh and nutritious food, they will stop all rumblings in your tummy and taste good too.

courgettes & cheddar
on toast

2 courgettes, grated

200 g mature Cheddar cheese, grated

1 shallot, finely chopped

1 small egg

a dash of Worcestershire sauce

4 slices of bread, toasted

sea salt and freshly ground black pepper

serves 4

Put the grated courgettes in a clean, dry tea towel and twist tightly, squeezing out all the excess liquid.

Transfer to a mixing bowl and add the cheese, shallot, egg, Worcestershire sauce, salt and pepper. Stir thoroughly.

Put the toasted bread onto a baking sheet, pile the courgette mixture on top and cook under a medium-hot grill until golden brown. Serve hot.

This Italian-inspired toasted sandwich is extremely versatile and makes a delicious and quick brunch or lunch dish. It takes only minutes to prepare and will keep you satisfied until supper time.

sardine bruschetta

120 g tinned sardines

1 teaspoon balsamic vinegar

1 slice of wholemeal bread, lightly toasted

1 tablespoon finely grated Cheddar cheese (optional)

3–4 cherry tomatoes, halved

serves 1

Preheat the gill to medium.

Put the sardines and balsamic vinegar in a bowl and mash with a fork. Pile the sardines on top of the toasted bread and sprinkle with the grated cheese, if using.

Transfer to a grill rack with the tomatoes and cook under the preheated grill for 2–3 minutes, or until the cheese is golden brown and the tomatoes are hot.

Put the tomatoes on top of the toast and cut it into fingers.

Fish cakes of any kind are perfect brunch brainfood, but these, made with sweet potatoes, are particularly good. Keep any leftover lemon and rosemary mayonnaise in the fridge for up to 3 days.

salmon & sweet potato fish cakes

500 g salmon fillets

1 tablespoon olive oil

500 g sweet potatoes, peeled and cubed

4 spring onions, finely chopped

1 small garlic clove, peeled and crushed

grated zest and juice of ½ lemon

50 g fine cornmeal

sunflower oil, for frying

sea salt and freshly ground black pepper

green salad, to serve

lemon and rosemary mayonnaise

leaves from 1 sprig of fresh rosemary

½ teaspoon sea salt

2 free range egg yolks

1 teaspoon Dijon mustard

300 ml olive oil

1–2 tablespoons freshly squeezed lemon juice

serves 4

Preheat the oven to 200°C (400°F) Gas 6.

Put the salmon fillets on a sheet of aluminium foil and drizzle with the olive oil. Wrap the foil loosely around the salmon and bake for 20–25 minutes. Remove from the oven and leave until cold. Flake the flesh with a fork, reserving any juices from the parcel.

Meanwhile, cook the potatoes in lightly salted, boiling water for 15 minutes. Drain well, return to the saucepan and dry out briefly over a low heat. Mash coarsely and set aside to cool.

Add the fish with the juices, spring onions, garlic, lemon zest and juice to the cooled potatoes. Season to taste and mix well. Shape into 8 small fish cakes and refrigerate for 30 minutes.

To make the lemon and rosemary mayonnaise, grind the rosemary leaves and salt to a powder with a mortar and pestle. Put in a food processor with the egg yolks and mustard and blend briefly. With the motor running, gradually add the oil through the funnel until thickened and glossy. Add lemon juice to taste.

Coat the fish cakes with cornmeal. Put enough oil to cover the bottom in a frying pan and heat until hot. Add the fish cakes and fry for 4–5 minutes on each side until golden. Serve with the mayonnaise and a green salad.

This is such a classic sandwich and deservedly so, since it is really very delicious! Always use very fresh bread – all the better for soaking up those juices – and for this particular sandwich, unbleached bread is best.

steak & tomato sandwich

olive oil, for greasing

4 sirloin steaks, 100 g each

8 slices of bread

butter, for spreading

4 teaspoons Dijon mustard

2 beef tomatoes, sliced

2 bunches of rocket, about 100 g

sea salt and freshly ground
black pepper

serves 4

Heat a stove-top grill pan or a non-stick frying pan with a little olive oil. When very hot, add the steaks and cook to taste: 1 minute on each side for rare steak, 2 minutes each side for medium or 3 minutes each side for well done.

Meanwhile, spread 4 slices of the bread with butter and mustard, then add the sliced tomatoes and rocket.

Top with the cooked steak and sprinkle with seasoning. Butter the remaining slices of bread and put them on top of the steaks. Press together, wrap in a napkin to catch those drips and eat.

Indian salads or raitas almost always include yoghurt as the main element of the dressing, with toasted spices as the flavour note. Use almost any crisp fruit or vegetable in this salad – vary according to what's in season.

fruit & vegetables
with yoghurt dressing

4 tablespoons cashew nuts

4 small crisp lettuces, cut into wedges or torn into pieces

6 segments pomelo or grapefruit (preferably pink), membranes removed, segments pulled into 2–3 pieces (optional)

12 large red or white grapes, or both, halved lengthways and deseeded

6 red radishes, finely sliced

1 mini cucumber, halved lengthways, deseeded and thinly sliced

3 cm fresh ginger, peeled and thinly sliced

4 tablespoons flaked coconut, soaked in water if desiccated (optional)

sprigs of fresh coriander (optional)

yoghurt dressing

a pinch of lovage seeds (optional)

1 teaspoon mustard seeds

a pinch of crushed chillies

½ teaspoon salt

½ teaspoon sugar

3 cm fresh ginger, peeled

250 ml natural yoghurt

serves 4

To make the yoghurt dressing, put the lovage and mustard seeds and the chilli in a dry frying pan and toast over medium heat until aromatic. Transfer to a small bowl and leave to cool. Add the salt and sugar, then grate the ginger and squeeze the gratings into the bowl. Stir in the natural yoghurt.

Put the cashew nuts into the same pan and toast over medium heat until golden. Do not allow to burn. Remove from the heat, transfer to a small bowl and leave to cool. When cool, chop coarsely with a knife.

Put the lettuce wedges onto a plate, add the pomelo pieces, if using, grapes, radishes, cucumber and ginger. Spoon over the dressing sparingly. Sprinkle with the cashew nuts, coconut and coriander, if using.

Avocado is so creamy and delicious it can really be used as a dressing in itself. Avocado loves salty things, like seafood, smoked food and bacon. Share it for brunch with salad leaves, pancetta and a regular dressing.

avocado salad

6 very thin smoked pancetta or bacon slices, or about 200 g pancetta cubes

1 tablespoon olive oil

250 g salad leaves (a mixture of soft, crisp and peppery)

1–2 ripe Hass avocados

dressing

6 tablespoons extra virgin olive oil

1 tablespoon cider vinegar or rice vinegar

1 garlic clove, peeled and crushed

1 teaspoon Dijon mustard

sea salt and freshly ground black pepper

serves 4

If using pancetta, cut the slices into 3–4 pieces. Heat a frying pan, brush with the olive oil, add the pancetta and cook over medium heat, without disturbing the pancetta, until crisp on one side. Using tongs, turn the slices over and fry until crisp and papery but not too brown. Remove and drain on kitchen paper.

To make the dressing, put all the ingredients in a salad bowl and beat with a fork or small whisk. When ready to serve, add the salad leaves and turn in the dressing, using your hands. Cut the avocados in half and remove the stones. Using a teaspoon, scoop out balls of avocado into the salad. Toss gently if you like (though this will send the avocado to the bottom of the bowl). Add the pancetta and serve.

easy eggs

Perfect for a leisurely breakfast or brunch. Adding a drizzle of honey and a pinch of cinnamon to the tomatoes gives them an irresistibly warm, scented sweetness that goes perfectly with the smooth, creamy eggs and earthy, pungent rye.

creamy scrambled eggs on rye
with cinnamon-honey roasted tomatoes

3 plum tomatoes

¼ teaspoon ground cinnamon

1 teaspoon clear honey

½ tablespoon olive oil

4 eggs

1 tablespoon double cream

4 slices of light rye bread

20 g butter, plus extra for spreading

sea salt and freshly ground black pepper

serves 2

Preheat the oven to 220°C (425°F) Gas 7.

Cut the tomatoes in half lengthways and arrange in a baking dish, cut side up. Sprinkle with cinnamon and seasoning and drizzle over the honey and olive oil. Roast for 30 minutes, pouring any juices back over the tomatoes part way through cooking.

When the tomatoes are nearly cooked, put the eggs and cream in a bowl, season and beat briefly. Toast the rye bread in a toaster or under the grill and keep it warm.

Melt the butter in a small, non-stick saucepan over medium-low heat until sizzling. Pour in the eggs and cook gently for 1–2 minutes, stirring constantly, until thick and creamy. (The eggs will continue to cook after you remove the pan from the heat, so be careful not to overcook.)

Quickly butter the rye toast and put 2 slices on each plate. Spoon the scrambled eggs on top and pile 3 tomato halves on each portion. Spoon over any extra tomato juices, sprinkle with pepper and serve immediately.

note: Don't use dark, moist rye bread such as pumpernickel for this recipe. It doesn't toast well, and won't give the delicious crispness of a light rye.

Stirring a little creamy goats' cheese into lightly scrambled eggs transforms a simple dish into a delicious and rather special brunch. The nasturtium flowers are optional, but they do add a delightful flash of colour as well as a delicate peppery flavour.

creamy eggs
with goats' cheese

12 free range eggs

100 ml single cream

2 tablespoons chopped
fresh marjoram

50 g butter

200 g goats' cheese, diced

a handful of nasturtium flowers,
torn (optional)

sea salt and freshly ground
black pepper

toasted walnut bread, to serve

serves 4

Beat the eggs in a bowl with the cream, marjoram and a little seasoning. Melt the butter in a non-stick saucepan, add the eggs and stir over low heat until they are beginning to set.

Stir in the goats' cheese and continue to cook briefly, still stirring, until the cheese melts into the eggs. Add the nasturtium flowers, if using, and spoon onto the toast. Serve immediately.

Parma ham, sautéed so it becomes really crisp, adds a lovely texture to the creamy sauce and egg yolks. Try substituting smoked salmon for the ham or, for a vegetarian version, replace the ham with wilted spinach as in the Eggs Florentine on page 121.

eggs benedict
on toasted muffins

4 large Parma ham slices

4 eggs

1 tablespoon vinegar
(preferably distilled)

4 English muffins

hollandaise sauce

250 g unsalted butter

3 egg yolks

1 teaspoon freshly squeezed
lemon juice

sea salt and freshly ground
black pepper

serves 4

To make the hollandaise sauce, put the butter in a small saucepan and melt it gently over very low heat, without letting it brown. Put the egg yolks, 2 tablespoons water, and lemon juice in a blender and process until frothy. With the blade turning, gradually pour in the melted butter in a steady stream until the sauce is thickened and glossy. Transfer the sauce to a bowl set over a saucepan of hot water. Cover and keep the sauce warm.

Grill or sauté the slices of Parma ham until really crisp and keep them warm in a low oven. To poach the eggs, bring a saucepan of lightly salted water to the boil. Add the vinegar and reduce to a gentle simmer. Swirl the water well with a fork and crack 2 eggs into the water. Cook for 3 minutes, remove with a slotted spoon and repeat with the remaining 2 eggs.

Meanwhile, toast the muffins whole and top each with a slice of crisp Parma ham. Put the poached eggs on top of the ham. Spoon over the hollandaise, sprinkle with seasoning, and serve at once.

If you haven't the time or inclination to make your own, you can buy excellent ready-made hollandaise sauce in large supermarkets, taking all the hassle out of making this divine breakfast. A good-quality cheese sauce works just as well.

eggs florentine
on toasted muffins

2 eggs

1 tablespoon vinegar (preferably distilled)

1 tablespoon butter, plus extra to spread

200 g baby spinach

a pinch of freshly grated nutmeg

2 English muffins

2–4 tablespoons Hollandaise Sauce (page 118)

sea salt and freshly ground black pepper

serves 2

To poach the eggs, bring a saucepan of lightly salted water to the boil. Add the vinegar and reduce to a gentle simmer. Swirl the water well with a fork and crack the eggs into the water. Cook for 3 minutes and remove with a slotted spoon.

Meanwhile, melt the butter in a saucepan, then add the spinach. Cook for about 3 minutes, stirring occasionally, until the spinach begins to wilt. Season with nutmeg and salt and pepper. Remove from the heat, cover and keep it warm.

Toast the muffins whole and spread with butter. Spoon some spinach onto each muffin (taking care to drain off any excess liquid as you do so). Set an egg on top, spoon over the hollandaise sauce, sprinkle with a little more pepper and serve immediately.

Smoked salmon and eggs is one of those combinations that works at any time of day. This is an easy, elegant dish that takes no time at all and makes the perfect breakfast treat. Surprise someone special with this breakfast in bed.

baked eggs
with smoked salmon & chives

250 g smoked salmon slices, chopped

1 tablespoon snipped fresh chives

4 eggs

4 tablespoons double cream

freshly ground black pepper

freshly made toast, to serve

4 shallow ovenproof dishes or ramekins, well greased

serves 4

Preheat the oven to 180°C (350°F) Gas 4.

Divide the smoked salmon and chives between the 4 dishes. Make a small indent in the salmon with the back of a spoon and break an egg into the hollow. Sprinkle with a little pepper and spoon the cream over the top.

Put the ramekins in a roasting tin and half-fill the tin with boiling water. Bake for 10–15 minutes, or until the eggs have just set. Remove from the oven, leave to cool for a few minutes, then serve with toast.

When time is short, but something warm and comforting is nevertheless required, these baked eggs go down a treat. The spinach adds both colour and a healthy mineral kick. Very little effort is required but the results are delicious.

eggs cocotte

60 g fresh spinach, chopped

4 eggs

4 tablespoons milk

75 g Parmesan cheese, grated

sea salt and freshly ground black pepper

4 ovenproof ramekins, greased

serves 4

Preheat the oven to 200°C (400°F) Gas 6.

Divide the spinach between the prepared ramekins. Crack an egg on top, add a spoonful of milk to each, then season and top with the Parmesan. Put the ramekins on a baking sheet in the preheated oven and cook for 6 minutes.

Tea-smoked salmon replaces the more traditional smoked haddock in this version of the classic Anglo-Indian breakfast dish. It is a substantial meal, perfect for when you've got a big day ahead of you.

kedgeree
with tea-smoked salmon

40 g butter

1 onion, finely chopped

250 g basmati rice

1 tablespoon curry paste

4 cardamom pods, crushed

1 cinnamon stick, crushed

1 teaspoon ground turmeric

600 ml fish or vegetable stock

2 hard-boiled eggs, peeled and quartered

chopped fresh chives and parsley, to serve (optional)

sea salt and freshly ground black pepper

tea-smoked salmon

500 g salmon fillet

8 tablespoons rice

8 tablespoons tea leaves

8 tablespoons soft brown sugar

serves 6

Melt the butter in a saucepan, add the onion and fry gently for 5 minutes. Add the rice, curry paste and spices, stir once, then add the stock. Bring to the boil, cover and simmer over very low heat for 20 minutes.

Meanwhile, to smoke the salmon, cut the fillet into 4 equal pieces and sprinkle with seasoning. Line a wok with a sheet of aluminium foil and put the rice, tea leaves and sugar in the bottom. Arrange a rack over the top. Cover and heat for 5–8 minutes, until the mixture starts smoking. Slide the fish fillets, skin-side down, onto the rack, cover and smoke over high heat for 4 minutes. Remove the wok from the heat but leave undisturbed for a further 3 minutes. Remove the fish and keep it warm.

Skin and flake the salmon into large pieces and add to the spiced rice. Season to taste and mix briefly with a fork. Cover and leave for 5 minutes. Serve topped with the egg quarters and sprinkled with the chopped herbs.

This creamy, light topping is packed with the flavour of asparagus. For the best results, make this with the freshest asparagus. If you have some, you can drizzle a little truffle oil over for a special occasion, as the flavours of eggs and truffle go very well together.

egg, mascarpone & asparagus
crostini

1 Italian *sfilatino* or thin French baguette, sliced into thin rounds

extra virgin olive oil, for brushing

125 g unsalted butter, softened

4 tablespoons chopped fresh parsley

4 spring onions, finely chopped

12 spears of fresh green asparagus, stems trimmed

6 large eggs

4–6 tablespoons mascarpone cheese, softened

truffle oil, for drizzling (optional)

sea salt and freshly ground black pepper

serves 6

Preheat the oven to 190°C (375°F) Gas 5.

To make the crostini, brush both sides of each slice of bread with olive oil and spread out on a baking sheet. Bake for about 10 minutes until crisp and golden.

Meanwhile, beat the butter with the parsley and spring onions and season to taste.

Cook the asparagus in boiling salted water for about 6 minutes until tender. Cut off and reserve the tips and slice the stems.

Boil the eggs for 6–8 minutes. Plunge into cold water for a couple of minutes, then shell and roughly mash with a fork. Add the spring onion mixture and mascarpone and stir until creamy. Fold in the sliced asparagus stems, then season with salt and pepper.

Spread the egg mixture thickly onto the crostini, top with the asparagus tips and drizzle with a couple of drops of truffle oil, if using, or some extra virgin olive oil.

Even as an adult you never tire of dunking toast into the perfect soft-boiled egg. It's even better when you dip in asparagus spears. Remember the eggs need to be at room temperature before they are plunged into boiling water.

boiled eggs
with asparagus soldiers

24 thick asparagus spears

8 large eggs, at room temperature

sea salt and freshly ground black pepper

freshly made toast, to serve

serves 4

Tie the asparagus into bunches of 6 with string. Steam or boil them for 3–4 minutes, or until just tender. Drain and keep them warm.

Meanwhile, cook the eggs in gently boiling water for 4 minutes, then transfer them to eggcups. Remove the tops of the eggs with a spoon and season to taste. Serve with toast and the asparagus.

Ever since this dish began cropping up in south-western diners, huevos rancheros has become as mainstream as omelettes on menus across the country. You can use shop-bought salsa for this but be sure to use the cooked variety instead of raw.

huevos rancheros

4 corn tortillas

3 tablespoons vegetable oil

60 g mild Cheddar cheese, grated

4 eggs

sea salt and freshly ground pepper

salsa

6 plum tomatoes, halved

2 jalapeño peppers

8 garlic cloves, unpeeled

4 tablespoons chopped
fresh coriander

1 teaspoon Tabasco Sauce or
favourite hot sauce

1 small red onion, finely chopped,
to serve

serves 4

To make the salsa, place the halved tomatoes cut-side up in a shallow roasting tin. Season and place on the top rack under a preheated grill. Grill for about 10 minutes, or until charred.

Preheat the oven to 200°C (400°F) Gas 6.

Meanwhile, in a dry, non-stick frying pan, char the peppers and garlic cloves. Keep turning to colour all sides. When done, peel the garlic and place in a food processor. Put the peppers in a plastic bag, tie a knot in the bag and leave the peppers to steam for a few minutes, then peel, deseed and stem. Add the flesh to the food processor along with the tomatoes, 2 tablespoons of the coriander and the Tabasco. Season and pulse until smooth. Pour into a saucepan and cook briefly over medium heat to warm through.

Brush the tortillas with 2 tablespoons of the oil and bake for 5 minutes until golden. Divide the cheese between the tortillas and return to the oven for 5 minutes until the cheese has melted. Turn off the oven, open the door and leave the tortillas in to keep warm. Fry the eggs in a non-stick frying pan in the remaining tablespoon of oil. Place the tortillas on 4 plates and slip an egg on top of each. Spoon the warm salsa over each and sprinkle with the chopped onion and remaining coriander.

This classic tortilla consists of just three ingredients: eggs, potatoes and onions. Together, they are transformed into an unbelievably delicious dish. Tortillas may be cut into squares or wedges or even between chunks of bread – a favourite way in Spain.

classic spanish tortilla

1 large onion

3–4 tablespoons extra virgin olive or sunflower oil

4 potatoes, about 500 g, peeled

5 large eggs

sea salt and freshly ground black pepper

a 20-cm heavy, non-stick frying pan (measure the base, not the top)

serves 2–3

Cut the onion in half, then slice thinly lengthways and separate into slivers. Heat 3 tablespoons of the oil in the frying pan.

Thinly slice the potatoes, then add them to the pan in layers, alternating with the onion. Cook for 10–15 minutes over medium-low heat, lifting and turning occasionally, until just tender. The potatoes and onions should not brown very much.

Meanwhile, break the eggs into a large bowl, whisk briefly with a fork and season. Remove the potatoes and onions from the pan and drain, reserving any oil. Add the vegetables to the bowl of eggs and mix gently.

Heat the reserved oil in the pan, adding a little extra if necessary. Add the potato and egg mixture, spreading it evenly in the pan. Cook over medium-low heat until the bottom is golden brown and the top almost set.

Put a plate or flat saucepan lid on top of the pan and invert the pan so the tortilla drops onto the plate or lid. Return to the pan, brown-side up, and cook on top of the stove for 2–3 minutes until the other side is lightly browned. Turn again and transfer to a serving plate, with the most attractive side upwards. Serve hot or at room temperature, cut into wedges.

This is a great way to cook an omelette – once prepared, it can finish cooking in the oven, making the whole thing quite relaxed. It is ideal for a late, lazy breakfast, but good enough to eat at any time of the day. Make sure the pan handle is ovenproof.

baked brunch omelette

2 tablespoons sunflower oil

4 slices of smoked bacon,
cut into strips

1 onion, finely sliced

1 medium potato, cubed

75 g button mushrooms, sliced

5 large eggs

90 ml milk

75 g mature Cheddar cheese, grated

1 tablespoon unsalted butter

1 tablespoon freshly grated
Parmesan cheese

sea salt and freshly ground
black pepper

*a 20-cm heavy, non-stick frying pan
(measure the base, not the top)*

serves 2–3

Preheat the oven to 200°C (400°F) Gas 6.

Heat the sunflower oil in the frying pan, add the bacon, onion and potato and fry for 6 minutes, or until the potatoes start to brown. Add the mushrooms and fry for 2 minutes.

Meanwhile put the eggs and milk in a large bowl and whisk briefly with a fork, just enough to mix the yolks and whites. Season with salt and plenty of pepper. Stir in three-quarters of the Cheddar.

Using a slotted spoon, transfer the potato mixture to the bowl of eggs and mix well. Add the butter to the frying pan and, when it starts to foam, pour in the omelette mixture. Sprinkle with the remaining cheese and transfer to the preheated oven.

Cook for 12–15 minutes, or until just set. Loosen the edges with a spatula or palette knife and slide onto a warmed serving plate. Sprinkle with Parmesan, cut into wedges and serve immediately.

Loaded with sausages, fried potatoes and onions, this dish is perfect comfort food. Ring the changes with different kinds of sausage – try slices of chorizo, cubes of black pudding or *morcilla* (traditionally Spanish), spicy Italian sausages or even frankfurters.

sausage, potato & onion tortilla

3–4 tablespoons extra virgin olive or sunflower oil

6 pork chipolata sausages with herbs

1 onion

3 potatoes, about 325 g, thinly sliced

5 large eggs

sea salt and freshly ground black pepper

a 20-cm heavy, non-stick frying pan (measure the base, not the top)

serves 2–3

Heat 1 tablespoon of the oil in the frying pan. Add the sausages and fry for 8–10 minutes, turning them frequently. Remove and set aside. Wipe out the pan with kitchen paper.

Cut the onion in half and then into slivers lengthways.

Heat 2 tablespoons of the oil in the cleaned pan. Add the potatoes, layering them with the onions. Cook for 10–15 minutes over medium-low heat, lifting and turning occasionally, until just tender. The potatoes and onions should not brown very much.

Meanwhile, break the eggs into a large bowl, add seasoning and whisk briefly with a fork. Remove the potatoes and onions from the pan with a slotted spoon and add to the egg mixture. Thickly slice the sausages and mix with the eggs and potatoes.

Return the frying pan to the heat, adding a little more oil if necessary. Add the potato and egg mixture spreading it evenly. Cook over medium-low heat until the bottom is golden brown and the top has almost set.

Put a plate or flat saucepan lid on top of the pan and invert the pan so the tortilla drops onto the plate or lid. Slide back into the pan, brown-side up, and cook for 2–3 minutes until lightly browned underneath. Serve hot or warm, cut into wedges.

Baby spinach is essential for this recipe because the leaves wilt and soften quickly, so you needn't remove the stalks or chop the leaves. The pancetta adds a special depth of flavour. Like all frittatas, any leftover can be taken on a picnic or for a packed lunch.

spinach & pancetta frittata

6 large eggs

1 tablespoon extra virgin olive or sunflower oil

125 g smoked pancetta, cut into cubes, or smoked bacon lardons

4 spring onions, chopped

1 garlic clove, peeled and finely chopped

175 g baby spinach

sea salt and freshly ground black pepper

a 24-cm heavy frying pan (measure the base, not the top)

serves 4

Break the eggs into a bowl and whisk briefly with a fork. Season well.

Heat 1 tablespoon of the oil in the frying pan. Add the pancetta and cook over medium heat for 3–4 minutes until they start to brown.

Add the spring onions, garlic and spinach and stir-fry for 3–4 minutes or until the spinach has wilted and the onions have softened.

Pour the egg mixture into the pan, quickly mix into the other ingredients and stop stirring. Reduce to a low heat and cook for 8–10 minutes, or until the top has almost set. Slide under a hot grill to finish cooking the top. Serve hot or cold, cut into wedges.

Porcini are difficult to buy fresh, but are widely available dried. They are one of the best mushrooms, with an intense, rich flavour that will pervade the omelette. Strain their soaking liquid and add a spoonful to the omelette mixture, or keep it for a soup or stew.

porcini frittata

15 g dried porcini mushrooms

6 medium eggs

3 tablespoons mascarpone cheese

3 tablespoons chopped
fresh flat leaf parsley

3 tablespoons extra virgin olive
or sunflower oil

1 onion, halved and sliced

125 g button mushrooms, sliced

1 tablespoon freshly grated
Parmesan cheese

1 tablespoon unsalted butter

75 g fresh wild mushrooms

sea salt and freshly ground
black pepper

*a 20-cm heavy, non-stick frying pan
(measure the base, not the top)*

serves 2–3

Put the porcini in a small bowl and cover with warm water. Leave to soak for 30 minutes. Break 1 of the eggs into a bowl, add the mascarpone and mix well. Add the remaining eggs and whisk briefly with a fork. Stir in the parsley and season.

Heat 1 tablespoon of the oil in the frying pan, add the onion and cook over low heat until soft. Add another tablespoon of oil and the button mushrooms and cook for 5 minutes. Drain the porcini (reserving the soaking liquid) and chop if large. Add to the pan and cook for 2 minutes.

Using a slotted spoon, transfer the mushrooms and onions to the eggs and mix gently.

Wipe out the frying pan with kitchen paper, add the remaining oil and heat gently. Add the frittata mixture and cook over low heat until browned on the underside and nearly set on top. Sprinkle with Parmesan and slide under a hot grill to finish cooking the top and melt the cheese. Transfer to a warm serving plate.

Melt the butter in the frying pan, add the wild mushrooms and sauté quickly. Spoon over the top of the frittata and serve.

It is important to start folding the omelette while it is still slightly liquid in the centre to avoid it overcooking and becoming tough and leathery. Make sure the person who is going to eat it is ready first, rather than the omelette.

smoked salmon omelette

75 g smoked salmon, cut into thin strips

1 tablespoon milk

3 large eggs

2 teaspoons unsalted butter

2 tablespoons crème fraîche

1 tablespoon chopped fresh dill

sea salt and freshly ground black pepper

an 18-cm heavy omelette pan (measure the base, not the top)

serves 1

Put half the smoked salmon in a bowl, add the milk and leave to stand for 15 minutes.

Break the eggs into a bowl and whisk briefly with a fork. Season, then stir in the milk and smoked salmon.

Heat the butter in the omelette pan. When the butter starts to foam, pour in the egg mixture and cook over medium-high heat, drawing the mixture from the sides to the centre as it sets. Let the liquid flow and fill the space at the sides.

After a short time, the omelette will be cooked but still creamy in the centre. Top the omelette with the crème fraîche and sprinkle with chopped dill and the remaining smoked salmon.

Fold over one-third of the omelette to the centre, then fold over the remaining third, slide onto a warmed plate and serve immediately.

An ideal tasty brunch dish, especially for al fresco dining served with a crisp salad, this omelette is just bursting with Mediterranean flavours. It is worth buying tomatoes ripened on the vine for their extra taste explosion.

feta cheese & tomato
open omelette

5 large eggs

2 tablespoons chopped fresh basil

1 tablespoon chopped fresh mint

3 spring onions, finely chopped

2 tablespoons sunflower oil

75 g feta cheese, crumbled

8 small cherry tomatoes, halved

sea salt and freshly ground black pepper

an 18-cm heavy omelette pan (measure the base not the top)

serves 2

Break the eggs into a bowl and whisk briefly with a fork. Season, add 2 tablespoons water, the basil, mint and spring onions and mix briefly.

Heat the sunflower oil in the omelette pan. Pour in the egg mixture and cook over medium heat for 4–5 minutes, drawing the mixture from the sides to the centre until the omelette is half cooked.

Top with the feta and the tomato halves, cut-side up, and cook for 2 minutes. Slide under a preheated grill and cook until light golden brown. Slide onto a warmed plate and serve immediately.

A fusion of tortilla-inspired wraps with Portuguese-style piri-piri chicken which makes an even more filling alternative to standard omelettes. Increase or reduce the amount of piri-piri sauce in the marinade depending on how hot you would like it.

omelette wraps

2 tablespoons extra virgin olive oil

freshly squeezed juice of 1 lime

2 tablespoons chopped
fresh coriander

1 tablespoon piri-piri sauce, or other
hot sauce, such as harissa

2 skinless chicken breasts, about
150 g each, cut into thin strips

5 medium eggs

2 tablespoons milk

2 tablespoons snipped fresh chives

1 avocado, halved, stoned,
peeled and chopped

6 cherry tomatoes, quartered

4 teaspoons unsalted butter

sea salt and freshly ground
black pepper

*an 18-cm heavy omelette pan
(measure the base not the top)*

serves 2

Put the olive oil, lime juice and coriander in a bowl and mix with a fork. Put half the mixture in a shallow dish, add the piri-piri sauce and mix well. Add the chicken and stir to coat with the marinade. Set aside for 30 minutes.

Break the eggs into a bowl, then add the milk and some seasoning. Whisk briefly with a fork. Mix in the chives. Add the avocado, cherry tomatoes, the remaining olive oil and lime juice and stir gently to coat.

Stir-fry the chicken in a non-stick frying pan for 3–4 minutes, or until the juices run clear, then remove from the heat and set aside.

Meanwhile melt half the butter in the omelette pan over medium-high heat and swirl it around to coat the bottom and sides of the pan. When the butter starts to foam, pour in half the eggs.

Tip the pan to spread the eggs evenly over the base, leave for about 5 seconds, then draw the edges of the eggs to the centre, letting the liquid egg flow to the sides. When the omelette has just set, transfer to a warm plate, add the remaining butter to the pan and cook the second omelette in the same way.

Mix the cooked chicken with the avocado and tomatoes and divide between the two omelettes, spooning the mixture in a line down the middle. Roll up the omelettes, cut in half and serve.

fresh from the oven

This recipe is inspired by the little custard tarts (*pasteis de nata*) found all over Portugal. These divine little tarts make an ideal sweet treat for mid-morning, served with a shot of the strong but fragrant cardamom coffee.

baby custard tarts
with cardamom coffee

300 g sweet shortcrust pastry, thawed if frozen

300 ml milk

75 g caster sugar

1 teaspoon vanilla extract

2 egg yolks

1 whole egg

½ tablespoon cornflour

ground cinnamon, to dust

cardamom coffee

3 cardamom pods

4 tablespoons espresso coffee beans

a 7.5-cm biscuit cutter (optional)

two 12-hole mini-muffin tins

baking beans (optional)

makes 24 small tarts

Preheat the oven to 200°C (400°F) Gas 6.

Roll out the pastry on a lightly floured surface. Using a biscuit cutter or an upturned glass, stamp out 24 rounds about 7.5 cm across. Press the rounds carefully into the muffin tins, lightly prick the pastry bases and line each with a circle of greaseproof paper.

Fill the cases with baking beans (or rice if you don't have baking beans) and bake for 5 minutes. Remove the paper and beans and return to the oven for a few more minutes to crisp. Set aside and reduce the oven temperature to 150°C (300°F) Gas 2.

Meanwhile, to make the filling, put the milk, sugar and vanilla extract in a saucepan and bring to the boil. Simmer until reduced by about half.

Put the egg yolks, whole egg and cornflour in a bowl and beat well. Gradually beat in the vanilla milk. Pour the mixture into the pastry cases and bake for 10 minutes, until the surface of the custard is glossy and the centres are just set. Set aside until cold.

To make the coffee, remove the seeds from the cardamom pods and grind with the coffee beans, in a coffee grinder. Use the ground cardamom coffee to make espresso in the normal way.

Dust the tarts with cinnamon and serve with a small cup of the coffee.

Seville orange marmalade – everyone's favourite breakfast preserve – makes a delicious main ingredient for these simple muffins. Eat them shortly after they have come out of the oven, when they are still warm – they melt in the mouth.

marmalade muffins

150 g plain flour

150 g wholemeal flour

1 tablespoon baking powder

a large pinch of sea salt

1 large egg, lightly beaten

280 ml milk

2 teaspoons freshly squeezed orange juice

4 tablespoons vegetable oil or melted butter

150 g thick-cut Seville orange marmalade

a deep 12-hole muffin tin, well greased

makes 12 muffins

Preheat the oven to 220°C (425°F) Gas 7.

Sift the dry ingredients in a large bowl, mix thoroughly, then make a well in the centre. Add the egg, milk, orange juice and oil. Stir the marmalade to break up any large clumps, then add to the bowl. Mix quickly to form a coarse, slightly streaky batter. Do not beat or overmix or the muffins will be tough and dry. Spoon the mixture into the prepared muffin tin, filling each hole about two-thirds full.

Bake for 20 minutes, or until lightly browned and firm to the touch. Leave to cool in the tin for 1 minute, then turn out onto a wire rack. Eat warm. The muffins should be eaten within 24 hours or left to cool, then frozen for up to 1 month.

Everyone loves a blueberry muffin. These are extra special as they are packed with ground almonds and flavoured with lemon zest and juice to make them slightly tangy. Use wild berries if you can find them.

lemon, almond & blueberry muffins

50 g whole blanched almonds

250 g plain flour, sifted

1 tablespoon baking powder, sifted

85 g golden caster sugar

grated zest of 1 unwaxed lemon

1 large egg

280 ml milk

2 teaspoons freshly squeezed lemon juice

4 tablespoons vegetable oil

150 g fresh or frozen blueberries (if frozen, use them straight from the freezer)

a deep 12-hole muffin tin, well greased

makes 12 muffins

Preheat the oven to 200°C (400°F) Gas 6.

Put the almonds in a food processor and grind to a coarse meal. They should have more texture than commercially ground almonds. Transfer to a large bowl and mix with the flour, baking powder, sugar and lemon zest.

Lightly beat the egg with the milk, lemon juice and vegetable oil. Add to the dry ingredients and stir just enough to make a coarse, lumpy mixture. Add the blueberries and mix quickly, using as few strokes as possible, leaving the mixture slightly streaky. Do not beat or overmix or the muffins will be tough and dry.

Spoon the mixture into the prepared muffin tin, filling each hole about two-thirds full. Bake for 20–25 minutes, or until golden and firm to the touch. Leave to cool in the tin for 1 minute, then turn out onto a wire rack. Eat warm. The muffins should be eaten within 24 hours or left to cool, then frozen for up to 1 month.

Fresh peaches make these muffins special. Serve warm with Greek yoghurt or low-fat fromage frais. With their fresh fruit, oats and optional side serving of yoghurt, these bakes really are a complete breakfast in a muffin.

fresh peach & oat muffins

115 g rolled oats

300 ml buttermilk

1 large egg, lightly beaten

6 tablespoons melted butter or vegetable oil

85 g light muscovado sugar

200 g plain flour

1 teaspoon baking powder

½ teaspoon bicarbonate of soda

½ teaspoon ground cinnamon

¼ teaspoon grated nutmeg

2 almost ripe, medium peaches, stoned and flesh cut into large chunks

Greek yoghurt or low-fat fromage frais, to serve (optional)

a deep 12-hole muffin tin, well greased

makes 12 muffins

Preheat the oven to 220°C (425°F) Gas 7.

Put the rolled oats and buttermilk in a large bowl and leave to soak for 10 minutes. Add the egg, melted butter and sugar and mix well.

Sift the flour, baking powder, bicarbonate of soda and spices onto the soaked oat mixture and stir briefly. Quickly fold in the chopped peaches. The batter should look slightly streaky. Do not beat or overmix or the muffins will be tough and dry. Spoon the mixture into the prepared muffin tin, filling each hole about two-thirds full.

Bake for 20–25 minutes, or until golden brown and firm to the touch. Leave to cool in the tin for 1 minute, then turn out onto a wire rack. Eat warm. The muffins should be eaten within 24 hours or left to cool, then frozen for up to 1 month.

Quick to make, these mouth-watering muffins can be baked several days in advance, then reheated in the oven briefly before serving. Use good-quality dark chocolate, chopped up, rather than chocolate chips, as it has a much better flavour and texture.

pecan & chocolate muffins

250 g self-raising flour

1 teaspoon baking powder

75 g pecan nuts, finely ground

125 g soft light brown sugar

1 egg

50 ml maple syrup

250 ml milk

50 g butter, melted

100 g plain chocolate, coarsely chopped into very small pieces

chopped pecan nuts, to decorate

a 12-hole muffin tin, lined with paper cases

makes 12 muffins

Preheat the oven to 200°C (400°F) Gas 6.

Sift the flour and baking powder in a bowl, then stir in the ground pecan nuts and sugar. Put the egg, maple syrup, milk and melted butter into a second bowl and beat well. Beat the syrup mixture into the dry ingredients, then fold in the chocolate pieces.

Spoon the muffin mixture into the paper cases in the muffin tin, and sprinkle the surface of each muffin with extra chopped pecan nuts.

Bake for 18–20 minutes until risen and golden. Leave to cool in the tin for 1 minute, then turn out onto a wire rack. Eat warm. The muffins should be eaten within 24 hours or left to cool, then frozen for up to 1 month.

An all-time family favourite – who can resist these gooey, sticky caramel buns filled with cinnamon and nuts? They are so irresistible that you could eat them at any time of day, but mid-morning with a fresh brew is the perfect occasion.

sticky buns

500 g strong white bread flour, sifted

1 teaspoon sea salt

40 g golden caster sugar

15 g fresh yeast

200 ml milk, lukewarm

50 g unsalted butter, melted

1 large egg, beaten

nut caramel filling

60 g unsalted butter, very soft

2 teaspoons ground cinnamon

50 g light muscovado sugar

100 g pecan nuts or walnut pieces

sticky topping

90 g light muscovado sugar

4 tablespoons double cream

a 22 x 28 x 4-cm baking or roasting tin, well greased

makes 12 buns

Mix the flour, salt and sugar in a large bowl and make a well in the centre. Crumble the fresh yeast into another bowl, add the milk and stir until blended. Pour the yeast liquid into the well, then work in enough of the flour to make a thick batter. Cover the bowl with a damp tea towel and leave until foamy, thick and bubbly – about 15 minutes.

Add the butter and egg to the yeast mixture and work in the rest of the flour to make a soft but not sticky dough. If it is too dry or too sticky, add extra water or flour, 1 tablespoon at a time. Turn out onto a lightly floured surface and knead thoroughly for 10 minutes. Return the dough to the bowl and cover with a damp tea towel or put the bowl in an oiled plastic bag. Leave to rise at normal room temperature until doubled in size – about 1½ hours.

Knock down the risen dough with your knuckles, then turn out and roll into a rectangle, about 40 x 25 cm. To make the filling, beat the butter until creamy, then beat in the cinnamon and sugar. Spread the mixture over the dough leaving a 5-mm border around the edges. Scatter the nuts over, then roll into a 40-cm-long roll. Cut into 12 equal pieces and space slightly apart in the tin, in 4 rows of 3. Cover and leave to rise as before until doubled in size – about 30 minutes (or chill overnight).

Preheat the oven to 200°C (400°F) Gas 6.

To make the topping, put all the ingredients in a small saucepan, bring to the boil, reduce the heat and simmer for 1 minute. Pour the hot mixture over the buns. Bake for 25–30 minutes until golden and firm. Leave to cool in the tin for 10 minutes, then turn out carefully – the caramel will be hot. Leave to cool on a wire rack. Eat warm or at room temperature, within 24 hours.

Lazy weekend breakfasts are so good – it's that special feeling when time seems to stand still and the fast pace of weekday life slows right down. Why not start the day with a cup of tea or coffee in bed to gently wake you from your slumber, then head to the kitchen to create one of these extra-special breakfasts?

plum pastries

1 tin chilled ready-to-bake croissant dough, about 250 g

6 plums, halved and stoned

4 teaspoons honey

1 tablespoon flaked almonds

makes 6 pastries

Preheat the oven to 180°C (350°F) Gas 4.

Remove the dough from the tin, unravel it and flatten. Cut along the perforations to make 6 rectangles and lay well apart on a greased baking sheet.

Put 2 halves of fruit on each piece of pastry, then drizzle with honey and sprinkle with the almonds.

Bake for 15–20 minutes until puffed and golden. Remove from the oven and serve hot or cold.

These rich, dark, chocolatey cakes studded with chocolate-covered coffee beans and topped with a creamy coffee butter frosting are simply divine. Dusted with grated chocolate, they look like a plateful of mini cappuccinos.

choca-mocha cupcakes

100 g dark chocolate

150 g butter, at room temperature

150 g caster sugar

2 eggs

2 tablespoons cocoa powder

100 g self-raising flour

2 teaspoons instant coffee, dissolved in 1 tablespoon boiling water

40 g chocolate-covered coffee beans

grated dark chocolate, to decorate

coffee butter frosting

100 g butter, at room temperature

200 g icing sugar, sifted

2 teaspoons instant coffee, dissolved in 1 tablespoon boiling water

a 12-hole muffin tin, lined with paper cases

makes 12 cupcakes

Preheat the oven to 180°C (350°F) Gas 4.

Melt the chocolate in a heatproof bowl set over a saucepan of simmering water or in a microwave, then set aside to cool.

Beat the butter and sugar together in a bowl until pale and fluffy, then beat in the eggs, one at a time. Stir in the melted chocolate and cocoa powder. Sift the flour into the mixture and stir in, then stir in the dissolved coffee, followed by the coffee beans.

Spoon the mixture into the paper cases and bake for about 20 minutes until risen and a skewer inserted in the centre comes out clean. Transfer to a wire rack to cool.

To decorate, beat the butter, icing sugar and dissolved coffee together in a bowl until pale and fluffy. Spread the mixture smoothly over the cakes and sprinkle with grated chocolate.

Here's a real treat for a special breakfast or one of those mornings when what you crave is a strong coffee, a slice of freshly baked cake and a sit-down. They are so pretty that they are particularly good if you are expecting a couple of friends round for elevenses.

mini gingerbreads

230 g self-raising flour

1 teaspoon bicarbonate of soda

1 tablespoon ground ginger

1 teaspoon ground mixed spice

¼ teaspoon freshly grated nutmeg

¼ teaspoon ground cloves

115 g unsalted butter, cubed

115 g black treacle

115 g golden syrup

115 g dark muscovado sugar

280 ml milk

1 large egg, beaten

a mini Bundt tin, greased, or
a 900-g loaf tin, greased and lined

makes 6 small Bundt cakes or
1 loaf cake

Preheat the oven to 180°C (350°F) Gas 4.

Sift the flour, bicarbonate of soda, ginger, mixed spice, nutmeg and cloves onto a sheet of paper, then tip into a food processor. Add the butter and process until the mixture looks like very fine crumbs.

Put the treacle, golden syrup, sugar and milk in a pan and heat gently until the sugar dissolves. Cool until lukewarm, then, with the processor on, pour the mixture through the feed tube. Add the egg in the same way and process until just thoroughly mixed.

Spoon the mixture into the prepared Bundt tin until the holes are equally filled and bake for 20 minutes, or until firm to the touch. Repeat with the remaining mixture until you have 6 Bundt tins. Alternatively, if you are using a loaf tin, bake for 45–60 minutes, or until a skewer inserted into the centre comes out clean.

Leave to cool for 15 minutes before unmoulding onto a wire rack. Store in an airtight container and eat within 5 days.

An old-fashioned coffee cake, designed to serve with a cup of coffee (not made with it). When you cut a slice of this lovely cake you reveal the layer of crunchy nut streusel hidden in the middle. A real treat.

traditional pecan
coffee cake

streusel

100 g finely chopped pecan nuts

4 tablespoons dark muscovado sugar

1½ teaspoons ground cinnamon

batter

250 g unsalted butter, softened

2 large eggs, at room temperature, beaten

150 g caster sugar

225 ml soured cream

300 g plain flour

½ teaspoon bicarbonate of soda

2 teaspoons baking powder

a good pinch of salt

icing sugar, to dust

a Bundt tin, 23 cm diameter, well greased, or a 900-g loaf tin, greased and lined

makes 1 Bundt cake or loaf cake

Preheat the oven to 180°C (350°F) Gas 4.

To make the streusel mixture, mix the pecans, sugar and cinnamon in small bowl and set aside.

To make the batter, put the butter, eggs, sugar and soured cream in a large bowl and beat with an electric mixer on medium speed until smooth and well blended.

Sift the flour, bicarbonate of soda, baking powder and salt onto the mixture and mix in gently.

Spoon half the batter into the prepared Bundt or loaf tin and spread it evenly with a rubber spatula. Sprinkle with half of the streusel mixture. Spoon the rest of the batter into the tin and spread evenly. Sprinkle with the remaining streusel, then gently press the mixture onto the surface of the batter with the back of a spoon.

Bake for 45–55 minutes or until a skewer inserted in the thickest part of the cake comes out clean. Remove the tin from the oven and leave to cool in the tin, on a wire cooling rack. Leave to cool completely, then invert onto a serving platter. Dust with icing sugar before serving.

Store in an airtight container and eat within 4 days.

Coffee and walnuts are wonderful together. Drizzling the nutty cake with a spiced coffee syrup leaves it deliciously moist and gooey. This cake is equally at home as a dessert for a dinner party as it is mid-morning for a quick treat.

walnut cake
with coffee syrup

6 eggs, separated

175 g caster sugar

175 g walnuts, finely ground

75 g day-old breadcrumbs

whipped cream, to serve

coffee syrup

300 ml strong black coffee

100 g caster sugar

3 star anise

a 23-cm springform cake tin, greased and base-lined

serves 8

Preheat the oven to 180°C (350°F) Gas 4.

Put the egg yolks in a large bowl, add 125 g of the sugar and whisk until pale. Stir in the ground walnuts and breadcrumbs. (The mixture will be very stiff at this stage.)

Whisk the egg whites in a separate bowl until soft peaks form, then gradually beat in the remaining sugar. Stir a large spoonful of the beaten egg whites into the cake mixture, then fold in the rest until evenly mixed. Spoon into the prepared cake tin and bake in the preheated oven for 35–40 minutes, or until risen and springy to the touch. Remove from the oven and leave the cake in the tin.

Meanwhile, to make the coffee syrup, put the coffee, sugar and star anise in a saucepan. Heat until the sugar dissolves, then boil for 5–6 minutes, or until syrupy. Leave to cool slightly.

Using a cocktail stick, spike the cake all over the surface, then drizzle with half the syrup. Set aside to cool slightly. Serve the cake still warm with lightly whipped cream and the remaining coffee syrup spooned around it in a pool.

Light and crumbly in texture and crammed with delicious fruit and nuts – irresistible. Use very ripe bananas for maximum flavour. This loaf also works well as a sweet treat for the children when they come home from school.

banana pecan loaf

125 g unsalted butter,
at room temperature

170 g golden caster sugar

2 large eggs, beaten

½ teaspoon vanilla extract

400 g very ripe bananas

100 g pecan nuts, coarsely sliced

250 g self-raising flour, sifted

a 1-kg loaf tin, greased and base-lined

makes 1 large loaf cake

Preheat the oven to 180°C (350°F) Gas 4.

Using an electric mixer or wooden spoon, beat the butter with the sugar until light and creamy. Gradually beat in the eggs and vanilla extract to make a fluffy mixture. Mash the bananas with a fork – they should be fairly coarse rather than a purée. Carefully fold in the mashed bananas, pecans and flour. Transfer the mixture to the prepared loaf tin and smooth the surface with a palette knife. Bake in the preheated oven for about 1 hour, or until golden and firm to the touch and a skewer inserted into the centre comes out clean.

Leave to cool in the tin for 5 minutes, then turn out onto a wire rack to cool completely. Serve warm or at room temperature, thickly sliced and spread with butter. The cake is best eaten within 3 days. It can be frozen for up to 1 month.

For a full tea flavour, use a strong variety such as a breakfast or Irish blend, or a rich malty Assam. Eat the loaf cake thickly sliced, warm or even toasted, with or without butter and jam. It really is good enough to eat on its own.

breakfast tea loaf

100 g shredded bran cereal

120 g dark muscovado sugar

130 g mixed dried fruit

175 ml strong tea, warm

30 g walnut pieces

100 g plain flour, sifted

1½ teaspoons baking powder

1½ teaspoons ground mixed spice

a 450-g loaf tin, greased and base-lined

makes 1 medium tea loaf

Put the cereal, sugar and dried fruit into a large bowl, add the warm tea, stir well, then cover and leave to soak for 30 minutes.

Preheat the oven to 180°C (350°F) Gas 4.

Add the remaining ingredients and stir with a wooden spoon until thoroughly mixed. (The cereal will disappear into the mixture.)

Spoon the mixture into the prepared loaf tin and smooth the surface with a palette knife. Bake in the preheated oven for about 45 minutes, or until firm and well risen and a skewer inserted into the centre comes out clean.

Leave to cool in the tin until lukewarm, then turn out and eat while still warm. Alternatively, turn out onto a wire rack to cool completely.

Eat within 4 days, or freeze for up to 1 month.

Great for a fast, simple breakfast – on its own or toasted and buttered. Cinnamon, raisins and nuts are a classic combination. Make this on the weekend and enjoy your homemade breakfast bread every morning for the next few days.

cinnamon raisin nut bread

650 g strong white bread flour

1½ tablespoons ground cinnamon

1 teaspoon sea salt

1 teaspoon light muscovado sugar

100 g unsalted butter, chilled and cubed

15 g fresh yeast

425 ml milk, at room temperature

100 g raisins

75 g walnut pieces, lightly toasted

makes 1 large loaf

Sift the flour, cinnamon, salt and sugar into a large bowl. Rub in the butter with your fingertips until the mixture looks like fine crumbs, then make a well in the centre. Crumble the yeast into a jug and whisk in the milk. Pour into the well and mix in enough flour to make a thick batter. Cover the bowl and leave until thick and foamy – about 20 minutes.

Work in the rest of the flour to make a soft but not sticky dough. If it is too dry or too sticky, add extra water or flour, 1 tablespoon at a time. Turn out onto a floured surface and knead thoroughly for 10 minutes, or until smooth and elastic. Return to the bowl, cover with a damp tea towel and leave to rise at normal room temperature until doubled in size – about 1½ hours.

Knock down the risen dough with your knuckles, then work in the fruit and nuts, kneading until thoroughly mixed. Shape the dough into an oval loaf about 25 x 15 cm. Put on a greased baking sheet, cover and leave to rise as before until doubled in size – about 45 minutes.

Preheat the oven to 220°C (425°F) Gas 7.

Bake in the preheated oven for about 35 minutes, or until the bread is nicely browned and sounds hollow when tapped underneath. Leave to cool on a wire rack. Eat within 4 days, or slice and toast. The cooled loaf can be frozen for up to 1 month.

To get the best results for this recipe (and to feel virtuous), use a good sugarless muesli with ingredients such as raisins, dates, wheat flakes, oat flakes, apples, apricots, hazelnuts, almonds and raisins.

muesli round

500 g strong white bread flour

100 g stoneground wholemeal flour, plus extra to dust

250 g unsweetened muesli

2 teaspoons salt

15 g fresh yeast*, crumbled

about 400 ml milk and water mixed, at room temperature

1 tablespoon honey

2 tablespoons vegetable oil

makes 1 large round loaf

*To use easy-blend dried yeast, mix one 7-g sachet with the two kinds of flour, the muesli and salt. Pour in all the liquids, then proceed with the recipe.

Put the flours, muesli and salt in a large bowl and mix well. Make a well in the centre.

Put the yeast and 3 tablespoons of the milk in a small bowl and cream to a smooth liquid. Stir in the rest of the liquid, the honey and oil, then pour into the well in the flour.

Gradually mix the dry ingredients into the liquid to make a fairly firm dough. If it seems dry or stiff, or there are dry crumbs in the bottom of the bowl, work in extra milk or water, 1 tablespoon at a time. If the dough sticks to your fingers, knead in extra white flour, 1 tablespoon at a time. The amount of liquid needed will depend on the muesli mix.

Transfer the dough to a lightly floured work surface and knead for about 5 minutes. Return the dough to the bowl, cover with a damp tea towel and leave at room temperature until doubled in size – 1–1½ hours. Turn out onto a lightly floured work surface and knead for 1 minute. Shape into a round loaf 20 cm across. Put on a greased baking sheet and score into 8 segments with a very sharp knife. Cover and leave to rise as before – about 1 hour.

Preheat the oven to 220°C (425°F) Gas 7.

Uncover the loaf and sprinkle with wholemeal flour. Bake in the preheated oven for 30 minutes, or until it sounds hollow when tapped underneath. Remove from the oven and transfer to a wire rack to cool.

Eat warm, spread with butter and lots of apricot preserve, pear and ginger jam or apple marmalade – a good start to the day. These are so good you'll wonder why you only ever ate scones at teatime!

apple buttermilk scone round

1 large cooking apple or 1–2 crisp tart eating apples (about 250 g)

200 g plain flour, plus extra to dust

80 g wholemeal flour

1 teaspoon bicarbonate of soda

75 g demerara sugar, plus extra to sprinkle

75 g unsalted butter, chilled and cubed

about 140 ml buttermilk, plus extra to glaze, or milk to glaze

makes 8 scones

Preheat the oven to 220°C (425°F) Gas 7.

Peel, core and coarsely chop the apple into 1-cm chunks. Mix the flours, bicarbonate of soda and sugar in a food processor. Add the butter and process until the mixture looks like fine breadcrumbs. With the machine running, add the buttermilk through the feed tube to make a soft but not sticky dough.

Turn out onto a floured surface and knead in the apple chunks to form a coarse and bumpy dough. Shape into a ball and put in the middle of a greased baking sheet. With floured fingers, pat into a 22-cm round. Brush lightly with buttermilk to glaze, then sprinkle with a little demerara sugar to give a crunchy surface. Using a sharp knife, score the round into 8 wedges. Bake in the preheated oven for 20–25 minutes, or until lightly golden and firm to the touch.

Remove from the oven and leave to cool on a wire rack. Eat warm, immediately or within 24 hours. The scones are also good split and toasted. They can be frozen for up to 1 month.

Scottish cooks are famous around the world for their baking skills, and scones are perhaps their finest achievement. Mashed potato is used to replace some of the flour here, giving a light, moist texture and the Parmesan and pancetta give an Italian twist.

golden potato scones
with parmesan & pancetta

4 slices of pancetta or bacon, about 50 g, cut into small pieces

150–175 g plain flour

2 teaspoons baking powder

½ teaspoon salt

50 g unsalted butter, cubed

125 g cooked mashed potato

50 g Parmesan cheese, cut into tiny cubes

1 teaspoon dried oregano

about 2 tablespoons milk

1 egg yolk, beaten, to glaze

a fluted 6-cm biscuit cutter

makes 10 scones

Preheat the oven to 220°C (425°F) Gas 7.

Heat a frying pan and dry-fry the pancetta for 5–6 minutes, or until crispy. Remove with a slotted spoon and leave to cool on kitchen paper.

Sift the flour, baking powder and salt together in a large bowl. Add the butter and rub in until the mixture resembles breadcrumbs.

Add the potato, Parmesan, oregano and cooked pancetta and mix well. Add enough milk to form a soft but firm dough, turn out onto a lightly floured work surface and knead briefly. Roll out the dough to 1.5 cm thick and, using the biscuit cutter, stamp out 6-cm rounds. Re-roll any trimmings and cut more rounds, to make about 10 in total.

Place the scones on a well-greased baking sheet, brush the tops with the beaten egg and bake for 10–15 minutes, or until golden brown and well risen. Leave to cool a little on a wire rack, then serve while still warm, spread with unsalted butter.

Hot or cold, these make a great snack either mid-morning or mid-afternoon. Top with cottage cheese, cream cheese, hummus, or sliced tomatoes and basil.

herby cheese swirls

150 g wholemeal flour

2 teaspoons baking powder

100 g unprocessed oat bran

30 g polyunsaturated margarine, cubed

125 ml milk

60 g low-fat Cheddar cheese, grated

1 tablespoon chopped fresh flat leaf parsley

2 tablespoons chopped fresh basil

2 teaspoons chopped fresh rosemary

to serve (optional)

low-fat cottage cheese

low-fat cream cheese

hummus

tomato slices and fresh basil leaves

makes 10 swirls

Preheat the oven to 200˚C (400˚F) Gas 6.

Sift the flour and the baking powder in a large bowl, then stir in the oat bran. Rub in the margarine using your fingertips. The mixture should resemble breadcrumbs. Make a well in the centre and add the milk and 2 tablespoons water. Mix lightly with a round-bladed knife, adding extra water if necessary, to make a soft, pliable dough. Do not overmix.

Turn the dough out onto a lightly floured surface and knead gently. Roll out to a rectangle about ½ cm thick. Scatter half the cheese and all the herbs evenly over the surface, then dampen the edges of the dough with water. Beginning from one long side, roll up the dough like a Swiss roll, to make a thick sausage shape. Carefully cut into 3-cm slices using a sharp knife, to make about 10 rounds.

Transfer the rounds to a baking sheet, spacing them well apart. Sprinkle with the remaining cheese and bake for 15–20 minutes, until golden. Serve hot or cold, either plain or with your choice of topping.

perfect preserves

This is a quintessentially British preserve, tart with lemon yet sweet and buttery. It is delicious on toast or freshly made scones. It is easy to make so long as you stir it very frequently and keep the heat low so that the water in the pan barely bubbles.

lemon curd

2 large unwaxed lemons

125 g unsalted butter, cubed

180 g caster sugar

3 eggs, beaten

two 225-g glass jars

makes 2 small jars

Finely grate the zest from the lemons into a heatproof bowl. Squeeze the juice and add that to the bowl with the butter and sugar.

Place the bowl over a pan of just-simmering water, making sure the water doesn't touch the base of the bowl. Stir until the butter melts, add the egg and, using a wooden spoon, stir for 10–15 minutes until the mixture thickens noticeably and takes on a translucent look.

For a very smooth preserve, strain the curd through a fine sieve into a measuring jug, then pot it into small, sterilized jars (see page 4). Cover with clingfilm or greaseproof paper when cold. It will keep for 15 days in the refrigerator.

variations

lime & cardamom curd

Substitute the zest of 3 large unwaxed limes and the freshly squeezed juice of 5 limes for the lemons above. Add ¼ teaspoon finely ground cardamom seeds to the butter and sugar as it melts.

passion fruit & lime curd

Use the zest of 1 large unwaxed lime, the freshly squeezed juice of 2 limes and the sieved pulp of 8 ripe passion fruit (heating the pulp gently in the microwave for a few seconds makes it easier to sieve). Add 1–2 teaspoons of the passion fruit seeds at the end for crunch.

Apricots make one of the most luxurious preserves of all. The apricot season is fairly short so this recipe using dried apricots is very useful. Dried apricots need soaking well, then long, slow cooking to soften them.

dried apricot conserve

**500 g dried apricots
(soaked weight 1 kg)**

freshly squeezed juice of 1 lemon

1 kg sugar

**50 g walnut halves broken into
4 pieces**

**2 tablespoons Amaretto liqueur
(optional)**

four 250-g glass jars

waxed paper discs

makes about 1 kg conserve

Cut the apricots in half, put in a large bowl, cover with cold water, add the lemon juice and set aside for 24 hours.

Strain off the juice into a measuring jug and make up to 1 litre with cold water. Put the fruit in a heavy pan, add the juice and water and simmer over low heat for 30 minutes or until quite soft. The fruit can be mashed at this stage or left in pieces.

Add the sugar and bring slowly to simmering point. Cook gently, stirring until dissolved. Increase the heat and boil hard for 10 minutes, add the walnut pieces and return to a fast boil.

Remove the pan from the heat and leave to stand while you test for set*. If the jam is not ready, put the pan back on the heat to boil for a few minutes longer and test again. Repeat this process if necessary and remember to take the jam off the heat while testing, because over-boiling will ruin it.

When setting point has been reached, add the Amaretto to the pan, return to the boil, stir and skim if necessary. Let the jam rest for 20 minutes, then stir well and ladle into sterilized jars (see page 4). Seal at once with waxed paper discs and lids or covers. Leave to cool, label and store in a cool, dark cupboard until required.

*testing for set

Before you start making jam, always put a saucer and 2–3 teaspoons in the refrigerator to cool. Boil the reduced preserve hard for 5 minutes, then take the pan off the heat and test for set. Take a teaspoon of the preserve, put it on the cold saucer in the refrigerator or freezer and leave for 5 minutes. Push it with a finger – if it offers resistance or crinkles, it is ready.

There is no boiling needed for this recipe, so you keep the taste of fresh raspberries. Commercially produced jam sugar is perfect for this – it has added pectin that helps the jam thicken to a soft set. Use 120 ml liquid pectin if you can't find this special jam sugar.

uncooked freezer
raspberry jam

750 g fresh raspberries

1 kg sugar with added pectin (sometimes known as jam sugar)

2 tablespoons freshly squeezed lemon juice

makes two 500-g pots

Tip the raspberries into a bowl and crush a bit with a potato masher. Stir in the jam sugar and lemon juice. Cover with clingfilm and heat on MEDIUM in the microwave for about 5 minutes, or until warmed through thoroughly.

Uncover and stir gently to dissolve the sugar, then leave to stand overnight. Alternatively, heat in a saucepan until the sugar has dissolved.

The next day, pot up into freezer containers and freeze – keep one pot in the refrigerator for breakfast tomorrow. After removing from the freezer, store the jam in the refrigerator. Thaw before using.

The beauty of this marmalade is that it can be made in small quantities at any time of the year, not just when Sevilles are in season. Cut the peel to suit your taste – thick or thin by hand, chunky or fine using a blender.

chunky lemon, lime & grapefruit
marmalade

1 unwaxed lemon

1 small unwaxed pink grapefruit

1 unwaxed lime

1 kg sugar

freshly squeezed juice of ½ lemon

three 250-g jars

waxed paper discs

makes 500–750 g marmalade

Scrub the fruit and prise out any stalk ends. Put in a pan and cover with 500 ml water. Set over low heat and cook until tender – 1½–2 hours. The fruit is ready when it 'collapses'. Lime zest is much tougher than other citrus peel, so you must make sure it is tender at this stage.

Transfer the fruit to a chopping board and leave until cool enough to handle. Cut in half, scrape out all the flesh and pips and add to the pan of water. Bring to the boil and simmer for 5 minutes. Cut the zest into strips, or put it in a blender and blend until chunky. Strain the water from the pips and flesh and return it to the pan, adding the chopped zest and the lemon juice. Discard the pips and debris.

Add the sugar to the pan and bring slowly to simmering point, stirring until the sugar has dissolved. Because the sugar content is high, this will take quite a long time. When the marmalade has become translucent, you will know the sugar has dissolved and you can increase the heat. Bring to the boil and boil rapidly until setting point is reached – 5–10 minutes.

Take the pan off the heat and test for set (see page 193). If the marmalade is not ready, put the pan back on the heat to boil for a few minutes longer and test again. Repeat this process if necessary and remember to take the pan off the heat during testing because over-boiling will ruin it.

When setting point has been reached, return to simmering point, then turn off of the heat. Skim with a perforated skimmer, stir well and leave to stand for 30 minutes. Stir and ladle into sterilized jars (see page 4), seal with waxed paper discs and cover with a lid.

Leave to cool, label and store in a cool, dark cupboard until required.

This is a robust jam that deserves a place alongside the zingiest of marmalades. Choose young pink rhubarb if possible, because it will give a lovely pink colour to the jam – green rhubarb tends to turn brown when cooked.

rhubarb & ginger jam

1.5 kg young rhubarb, pink if possible

1.5 kg sugar

grated zest and freshly squeezed juice of 1½ unwaxed lemons

30–45 g fresh ginger, peeled, to taste

three or four 250-g glass jars

waxed paper discs

makes about 1 kg jam

Wipe the rhubarb, trim it, cut into chunks and put in a bowl with the sugar, lemon zest and juice. Cover and leave to stand overnight.

Crush the ginger with a mortar and pestle or blender and add to the fruit and sugar. Transfer to a large saucepan and bring slowly to simmering point, stirring all the time to dissolve the sugar. Simmer gently until the fruit has softened, then increase the heat and boil rapidly for 5–10 minutes until setting point is reached (see page 193).

If the jam is not ready, put the pan back on the heat to boil for a few minutes longer and test again. Repeat this process if necessary and remember to take the jam off the heat while testing, because over-boiling will ruin it.

Skim with a perforated skimmer, stir well and leave to stand for 20 minutes. Stir and ladle into sterilized jars (see page 4), seal with waxed paper discs and cover with a lid. Leave to cool, label and store in a cool, dark cupboard until required.

variation: Rhubarb combines well with soft fruit such as blackcurrants, raspberries and strawberries, giving them more body and reducing the seediness of the fruit. Use half soft fruit and half rhubarb, and leave out the ginger.

Make sure you use only plump, firm fruit here. You can use green figs, but they should be peeled first. It is perfect with crusty bread and butter, brioche or toast for breakfast, but would also make excellent jam tartlets or Italian crostata.

italian fig conserve

1.5 kg firm black figs

freshly squeezed juice of 2 lemons

1.2 kg sugar

1 envelope of vanilla sugar, 7.5 g (optional)

three or four 250-g glass jars

waxed paper discs

makes 750 g–1 kg conserve

Wipe the figs and chop into tiny pieces. Put in a saucepan with the lemon juice and 200 ml water. Cook over low heat until soft – this may take about 20–30 minutes, but if the skins are not cooked until tender at this stage, they will be tough when boiled with the sugar. Add the sugar and cook over low heat until dissolved. Stir in the vanilla sugar, increase the heat and boil until setting point is reached (see page 193) – 5–10 minutes.

If the jam is not ready, put the pan back on the heat to boil for a few minutes longer and test again. Repeat this process if necessary and remember to take the jam off the heat while testing, because over-boiling will ruin it.

When setting point has been reached, skim with a perforated skimmer, stir well and leave to stand for 20 minutes. Stir and ladle into sterilized jars (see page 4), seal with waxed paper discs and cover with a lid. Leave to cool, label and store in a cool, dark cupboard until required.

variation: Try experimenting with peaches, nectarines and kiwi, though it may not be necessary to cook the fruit for so long.

Berries make a marvellous seedless jam – use sweet ones like strawberries and raspberries, blackberry-raspberry crosses like the Scottish tayberry or the Californian loganberry, then something sharp such as cranberries or red or blackcurrants.

red berry jelly

500 g strawberries

500 g raspberries or redcurrants

500 g loganberries or tayberries

500 g blackcurrants

freshly squeezed juice of 1 lemon

sugar or preserving sugar (see method)

a jelly bag or muslin

two or three 250-g glass jars

waxed paper discs

makes 500–750 ml jelly

Put all the fruit (no need to strip currants) in a large preserving pan with the lemon juice and 500 ml water and bring slowly to the boil. Part-cover with a lid and simmer until the fruit has softened – about 10–15 minutes. Transfer to a jelly bag or muslin suspended over a large bowl and leave to drip overnight.

Measure the juice into a clean preserving pan and, for every 600 ml of juice, add 450 g sugar. Set over low heat and bring to simmering point, dissolving the sugar, stirring all the time. When it has dissolved, increase the heat and boil hard for 5–10 minutes until setting point is reached (see page 193).

When setting point has been reached, skim with a perforated skimmer and stir well. Stir and ladle into sterilized jars (see page 4), seal with waxed paper discs and cover with a lid. Leave to cool, label and store in a cool, dark cupboard until required.

delicious drinks

On many mornings for a lot of people, a cup of coffee simply IS breakfast. Whether you belong to this minimalist school, or coffee is just one essential ingredient of a larger meal, do forgo a convenient but watery cup of instant and take the time to prepare it properly.

coffee

To really taste the full, fresh and interesting flavours coffee can offer, you must make it correctly. Whether you are making espresso (when hot water is forced under pressure through dark-roasted coffee to extract maximum flavour), or using some sort of filter, follow these four principles and you won't go far wrong:

1 Buy good-quality, freshly roasted whole beans and grind them only just before using. Store whole beans in a dark airtight container, in a cool cupboard rather than in the fridge.

2 How finely you grind them depends on what method you are using to make the coffee:

espresso (including in stove-top pots): finely ground

cafetière: coarsely ground

filter: (by hand, machine, drip pots or vacuum pots): medium-finely ground

jug: coarsely ground

3 Be precise in your measurements. Getting the proper proportion of coffee to water and allowing them to brew together for the right length of time ensures you extract

the most character and aromatic oils from the beans without the brew becoming bitter. To make weaker coffee, add hot water when it has brewed correctly, rather than using too few beans in the first place.

When making espresso, fill the coffee container to the brim and do not compress the grounds, but level them off gently, otherwise the water will not be able to get through it evenly. Fill with water to the mark or rivet (depending on the design of your espresso maker).

For filter coffee, use 2 tablespoons coffee per 180 ml water, and brew it for 6–8 minutes to extract the full flavour from the beans.

4 Pour the water onto the grounds when it is just off the boil. This is to coax the soluble flavours from the coffee rather than scalding it and turning it bitter. Middle Eastern coffee is the exception, since this is boiled. As a general rule, do not keep coffee warm on the heat or it will become bitter and stewed. Instead, wrap the jug or pot in a tea towel while it infuses to keep it warm. Do not reheat previously brewed coffee, for the same reason.

Tea is a real chameleon of a drink. From a fortifying cup of 'builders' tea' to a cleansing and almost spiritual cup of green tea, there are forms and flavours to suit everyone and all occasions. Many, justifiably, consider their morning incomplete without it.

tea

Whether you drink it with or without milk or lemon and sugar is a matter of choice and tea variety, but as with coffee, there are certain principles to follow to ensure you get the best flavour from your tea. Many tea varieties are now available in tea bag form. While some are of reasonable quality, proper leaf tea is in a different league. To guarantee the best cup, follow these guidelines:

1 Buy top-quality tea leaves and store them in an airtight container to maintain freshness.

2 Use a tea pot. Keep the pot clean by rinsing it in detergent-free hot water after use to prevent a build-up of tannin, which will spoil future brews. Do not wash it in the dishwasher.

3 Fill the kettle with freshly drawn cold water and boil it. Do not use reheated water as it contains less oxygen and will give the tea a stale taste.

4 Warm the tea pot with hot water, then empty it. This ensures the boiling water is not cooled when it hits the leaves, and encourages the leaves to open properly.

5 Allow 1 heaped teaspoon tea leaves per person and 1 for the pot. Let the tea brew, and stir before pouring. Steep green teas for 3 minutes, and black and oolong teas for up to 5 minutes. Longer than this and your tea will taste stewed. If you like it weaker, taste after 2 minutes, and then at 2-minute intervals until it suits. Pour into the cup through a strainer.

herbal & fruit teas

For those concerned about stimulants, but in need of a low-cal hot drink, caffeine-free alternatives in the form of herbal and fruit teas are also popular. Many of these have specific additional benefits for health and well-being, such as digestive mint, memory-sharpening rosemary and soothing camomile.

Many of us know the benefits of a citrus kick to get us going in the morning. When the sun is shining on a gorgeous summer day, make this refreshing Iced Lime Tea to accompany your al-fresco breakfast. When it is wet, windy and cold, swap it for a cup of Hot Lemon Tea instead.

iced lime tea

1 litre freshly made tea, lightly brewed

sugar, to taste

1–2 unwaxed limes, finely sliced

ice cubes

sparkling mineral water, lemonade or ginger ale

serves 4

Strain the tea into a jug, stir in enough sugar to taste, leave to cool, then chill. Put sliced limes into a serving jug, then half-fill it with ice cubes. Half-fill the jug with the cold tea, then top up with sparkling mineral water, lemonade or ginger ale, stir and serve.

hot lemon tea

1 unwaxed lemon

1 tablespoon honey

1 pot of tea

serves 1

Cut 2 slices off the lemon and squeeze the juice from the rest. Put the honey and sliced lemon into a large mug, add the lemon juice, then top with tea. Stir and drink.

When you have indulged in an especially hearty breakfast or brunch, finish it off with a cup of this supremely soothing Mint Tea. Mint aids the digestion, so will guarantee satisfaction with your meal.

mint tea

a large bunch of fresh mint

sugar or honey, to taste (optional)

1 tablespoon green tea (optional)

serves 1–4

Break the mint into large handfuls and put into a cafetière.

Pour over boiling water, leave to steep for 3–5 minutes, then press the plunger. Pour into tea glasses, add honey, if using, and a few fresh mint leaves, then serve. If using green tea, add it at the same time as the mint.

Any apples will do for this juice, but Granny Smiths produce the most beautiful green. The ginger is optional but utterly delicious. The apple is a good source of Vitamin C while the mint helps digestion and the ginger will calm an upset stomach.

minty ginger granny smith

4 Granny Smiths, cored but not peeled, then cut into chunks

a chunk of fresh ginger, peeled and sliced (optional)

4–8 sprigs of fresh mint

1 tablespoon freshly squeezed lime juice

serves 1

Blend half the apples in a juicer or blender (adding a little water if necessary to make the blades turn), then add the ginger, mint and lime juice. Finally, add the remaining apples.

Tisane is a French word which means an infusion of herbs, flowers or leaves, usually dried – a kind of tea, in other words. In early times, they were seen as cures for many ailments. A tisanière is a tall, lidded cup, with a strainer inside to hold the herb. If you don't have one, you can use a cafetière instead.

rosemary tisane

4–6 sprigs of fresh rosemary

1–2 teaspoons honey

serves 1–2

Put the rosemary and honey into a tisanière or cafetière and cover with boiling water. Leave to infuse for 5 minutes, then plunge or strain.

variations: Tisanes can also be made with camomile flowers, lemon balm, marjoram, sage, thyme and orange blossoms.

Fresh pineapple contains the enzyme bromelian, which helps with digestion so it's a good fruit to have as a juice at the start of the day. It makes short work of fats and proteins, so is very good for dieters. It is also soothing for sore throats, coughs and upset stomachs.

pineapple crush

1 large pineapple

freshly squeezed juice of 1 lemon

ice cubes

4 passion fruit (optional)

sugar or honey, to taste

serves 4

Put the pineapple and lemon juice in a blender or juicer and blitz. Pour into a jug of ice. Stir in the flesh and seeds of 3 passion fruit and top with the remainder. Depending on the sweetness and ripeness of the pineapple, you may like to add a little sugar or honey.

Orange juice used in juices and smoothies will help to extend more expensive fruits and their gentle acidity also develops the flavour. Use juice you have squeezed fresh from the oranges rather than commercial juice which is often pasteurized, destroying all the Vitamin C and replacing it with ascorbic acid.

blueberry & orange smoothie

freshly squeezed juice of 4 oranges

about 250 g blueberries

sugar (optional)

serves 1–2

Put the orange juice into a blender, add the blueberries and blend until smooth. Add sugar to taste, if using.

berry, apricot & orange slush

8 ripe apricots, halved and stoned, then coarsely chopped

8 strawberries, hulled and halved

freshly squeezed juice of 2 oranges

serves 1

Put the apricots, strawberries and orange juice into a blender and purée until smooth, adding water if needed. (If the mixture is too thick, add a little water and blend again.)

note: If you prefer, you can remove the apricot skins before blending. To do so, bring a saucepan of water to the boil, then blanch the apricots for about 1 minute. Remove the skin with the back of a knife.

Fruit and yoghurt drinks are packed full of goodness and vitality and could almost be served as a meal in themselves. When really ripe mangoes are unavailable, tinned mango purée, available from Asian stores, makes an easy alternative. But ripe fresh mangoes are best – they are good for the skin and for people with high blood pressure.

raspberry & rosewater lassi

250 g raspberries

4 tablespoons rosewater

300 ml natural yoghurt

2–3 tablespoons honey

12 ice cubes

serves 4

Put all the ingredients in a blender. Blend to a purée. If your blender doesn't crush ice, add it at the end.

mango, coconut & passion fruit shake

1 large mango, peeled, or 300 ml mango purée

6 large passion fruit, or 150 ml passion fruit juice

200 ml coconut milk

12 ice cubes

serves 4

Cut the mango flesh away from the stone. Coarsely chop the flesh and put into a blender. Cut the passion fruit in half and scoop the seeds into a sieve placed over a bowl. Use a spoon to press down the seeds and extract all the juice. Add the juice, coconut milk and ice cubes to the blender and purée until smooth and creamy. If your blender doesn't crush ice, add it at the end.

Even people with a dairy intolerance are often able to eat yoghurt, since it changes its structure during fermentation – it's marvellous for upset stomachs too – so this is a lovely, satisfying drink to fill you up for the morning.

red berry smoothie

about 250 g berries, such as strawberries, cranberries, redcurrants or raspberries (for a pink smoothie), or blackberries and blueberries (for a blue smoothie)

250 ml natural yoghurt

125 ml crushed ice

sugar or honey, to taste

serves 2–3

Put all the ingredients into a blender and work to a thin, frothy cream. If your blender doesn't crush ice, add it at the end. If the smoothie is too thick, add a little water and blend again.

Taste, then add sugar or honey if you prefer.

Either of these will make a refreshing breakfast alternative. The Banana and Honey Breakfast Smoothie is packed with calcium and fibre and very good for you. The Watermelon and Lime Slush is a real taste of summer sunshine.

watermelon & lime slush

red flesh from 1 round watermelon

a chunk of fresh ginger, grated

to serve

2 limes, cut into wedges

crushed ice

serves 4

Press the melon flesh and ginger through a juicer, then pour into a jug half full of crushed ice. Serve immediately in glasses with lime wedges.

banana & honey breakfast smoothie

250 ml milk

250 ml yoghurt

2 tablespoons crushed ice

1 tablespoon honey

1 banana

1 tablespoon wheatgerm

serves 2–4

Put all the ingredients into a blender and blend until smooth. If your blender doesn't crush ice, add it at the end. Add extra fruit if you wish.

These smoothies are fantastic because they will pep you up and their vibrant colours alone will put a smile on your face. Packed with fresh fruit, their lovely fresh, clean flavours will gently awaken your taste buds so they're a great way of making sure you and your family get the benefit of all the healthy nutrients that fruit contains.

carrot, apple & ginger smoothie

5 large carrots, peeled

5 apples, cored

2.5 cm fresh ginger, peeled

serves 2

Press all the ingredients through a juicer or blitz in a blender (with a little water if necessary to make the blades turn). Serve immediately.

raspberry, kiwi & blueberry smoothie

200 g raspberries, fresh or frozen (no need to thaw)

2 kiwis, peeled

200 g blueberries, fresh or frozen

200 ml milk

serves 2

Put everything in a blender and blitz until smooth. Adjust the consistency with more milk if you wish, and serve immediately.

Bananas and papayas won't juice effectively – their pulp is too dense – but they are definitely candidates for the blender treatment. Bananas are high in complex carbohydrates, very nourishing and good for your cholesterol levels.

banana & papaya smoothie

1 small papaya, peeled, deseeded and cut into chunks

1 banana, peeled and cut into chunks

about 6 ice cubes

125 ml yoghurt or water (optional)

1 tablespoon wheatgerm (optional)

serves 2–4

Put the papaya and banana into a blender with the ice and the yoghurt or water, if using. If your blender doesn't crush ice, add it at the end. Blend until smooth, then add the wheatgerm, if using, and extra water or yoghurt to form a pourable consistency, then serve.

variation: Blueberries and banana make a famously good combination. Blend them with ice, yoghurt and a dash of honey.

There is something decidedly decadent about a glass of fizz in the morning. It's an absolute must if you're going to treat yourself to brunch, particularly if it's a special occasion, such as a birthday or an anniversary. Even if it's not, why not totally spoil yourself with one of these cocktails based on sparkling wine?

campari fizz

6 shots Campari

3 teaspoons caster sugar

1 bottle chilled sparkling wine, 750 ml

serves 6

Pour the Campari into champagne flutes and stir ½ teaspoon sugar into each glass. Top up with sparkling wine and serve.

peach bellini

3 ripe peaches

1 bottle chilled Prosecco or sparkling wine, 750 ml

serves 6

Peel the peaches by plunging them into boiling water for 30 seconds. Refresh them under cold water and peel off the skin. Cut in half, remove the stone and chop the flesh.

Put the peaches into a blender, add a small amount of Prosecco and process to a purée. Pour into glasses, top up with the remaining Prosecco and serve.

mimosa

6 blood or ordinary oranges

1 bottle chilled sparkling wine, 750 ml

serves 6

Squeeze the oranges and divide the juice between 6 glasses. Top up with wine and serve.

When tomato juice is on the menu for breakfast, you clearly mean business. If you can't face alcohol this early in the day, make the Virgin Mary which is a safer breakfast option. Sometimes, however, you need a real kickstart – which is when you should mix the more potent, alcoholic recipe and get on with the rest of the day.

kickstarter bloody mary

5 lemons

200 ml vodka

7 cm white horseradish, freshly grated, or 1 tablespoon horseradish sauce

1 tablespoon Worcestershire sauce

1 teaspoon Tabasco sauce

lots of freshly ground black pepper

750 ml tomato juice, well chilled

4 celery sticks, with leaves, to serve

serves 4

Half fill a large jug with crushed ice. Cut one of the lemons into slices and squeeze the juice from the others. Add to the jug, together with all the other ingredients except the celery. Mix well. Serve in highball glasses with a celery stick.

virgin mary

300 ml tomato juice, well chilled

2 grinds of black pepper

½ teaspoon Tabasco sauce

2 dashes Worcestershire sauce

2 teaspoons fresh lemon juice

1 teaspoon horseradish sauce

2 celery sticks, with leaves, to serve

serves 2

Shake all the ingredients over ice and strain into a highball filled with ice. Garnish with a celery stick.

index

credits

Recipes

Louise Pickford
Fresh figs with ricotta & honeycomb
Panettone French toast with coconut milk
Sweet bruschetta with quince-glazed figs
Hash browns
Mushroom burgers
Homemade baked beans
Salmon & sweet potato fish cakes
Creamy eggs with goats' cheese
Eggs Benedict
Kedgeree
Baby custard tarts
Boiled eggs with asparagus soldiers
Pecan & chocolate muffins
Raspberry & rosewater lassi
Mango, coconut & passion fruit shake
Campari fizz
Mimosa
Peach bellini
Walnut cake
Warm compote with peaches, apricots & blueberries
Roasted mascarpone peaches
Baked eggs with smoked salmon & chives

Fran Warde
Winter dried fruit pot
Rhubarb & plum compote
Apple & pear compote
Plum & honey cup
Frozen berry yoghurt cup
Banana & granola yoghurt pot
Eggs cocotte
Raspberry, kiwi & blueberry smoothie
Carrot, apple & ginger smoothie
Fruit platter
House granola
Swiss muesli
Courgettes & Cheddar on toast
Steak & tomato sandwich
Plum pastries
Kickstarter bloody Mary

Linda Collister
Muesli bars
Breakfast kebabs
Breakfast doughnuts
Muesli round
Mini gingerbreads
Traditional pecan coffee cake
French toast
Marmalade muffins
Lemon, almond & blueberry muffins
Fresh peach & oat muffins
Sticky buns
Banana pecan loaf
Breakfast tea loaf
Cinnamon raisin nut bread
Apple buttermilk scone round

Kate Habershon
Blueberry soured cream pancakes
Poppyseed pancakes
Triple chocolate pancakes
Date & pistachio griddle cakes
Apple wholemeal waffles
Classic Belgian waffles
Morning-after breakfast waffles
Cornmeal & bacon breakfast stack
Raspberry waffles

Jennie Shapter
Classic Spanish tortilla
Sausage, potato & onion tortilla
Smoked salmon omelette
Porcini frittata
Spinach & pancetta frittata
Baked brunch omelette
Feta cheese & tomato open omelette
Omelette wraps

Susannah Blake
Creamy orange French toast
Macerated berries on brioche French toast
Toasted brioche with lemon cream & fresh raspberries
Melting cheese & ham croissants
Toasted bagels with cream cheese & smoked salmon
Creamy scrambled eggs on rye
Eggs Florentine
Choc-mocha cupcakes

Rachael Anne Hill
Kickstart kebabs
Extra oaty porridge
All-in-one-oats
Bacon, tomato & basil toasty
Herby cheese swirls
Sardine bruschetta

Maxine Clark
Tea-infused fruit compote
Sausage & bacon rolls
Uncooked freezer raspberry jam
Fluffy potato pancakes
Egg, mascarpone & asparagus crostini

Lindy Wildsmith
Dried apricot conserve
Chunky lemon, lime & grapefruit marmalade
Italian fig conserve
Red berry jelly
Rhubarb & ginger jam

Annie Nichols
Swiss rösti
Potato noodles
Golden potato scones

Clare Ferguson
Churros
Arepas with fruit batidas

Ben Reed
Virgin Mary

Celia Brooks Brown
Rarebit

Hattie Ellis
Text on coffee

Clare Gordon-Smith
Text on tea

Jane Noraika
Exotic fruit scrunch

Brian Glover
Lemon curd

Jennifer Joyce
Huevos rancheros

Elsa Petersen-Schepelern
Fruit & vegetables with yoghurt dressing
Avocado salad
Rosemary tisane
Blueberry & orange smoothie
Berry, apricot & orange slush
Red berry smoothie
Banana & papaya smoothie
Iced lime tea
Hot lemon tea
Mint tea
Minty ginger Granny Smith
Pineapple crush
Watermelon & lime slush

Photography

Key: a=above, b=below, r=right, l=left, c=centre.

William Lingwood
Pages 1, 3cl, 27, 36c, 37, 39, 40, 43, 44, 47, 48, 51, 60, 64, 68, 71, 73, 77, 85, 86, 97, 112l, 115, 120, 204l, 204r, 205, 211, 212, 215, 216, 219, 220, 224, 227, 231, 232, 240

Ian Wallace
Pages 6br, 7, 9, 12, 15, 28, 63, 67, 74, 81, 93, 105, 112r, 116, 119, 127, 131, 150c, 150r, 153, 161, 173, 223

Tara Fisher
Pages 112c, 113, 135, 136, 139, 140, 143, 144, 147, 148, 188c, 189, 192, 196, 199, 200, 203

Debi Treloar
Pages 2, 3cr, 6ac, 6acc, 6bcc, 8l, 16, 31, 70l, 70r, 101, 106, 165, 207, 208, 235

Philip Webb
Pages 3r, 59, 98, 150l, 151, 154, 157, 158, 162, 174, 177, 178, 182

David Brittain
Pages 4, 6al, 6cl, 6bl, 6ar, 6acr, 6bcr

Noel Murphy
Pages 5, 23, 82, 102, 195

Peter Cassidy
Pages 20, 55, 109, 110, 123

Caroline Arber
Pages 11, 19, 124, 228

Nicky Dowey
Pages 24, 32, 90, 186

Francesca Yorke
Pages 8c, 8r, 36l, 188r

Martin Brigdale
Pages 52, 132, 166

Peter Myers
Pages 89, 94, 185

Polly Wreford
Pages 6bc, 35, 78

Jean Cazals
Pages 70c, 204c

Diana Miller
Pages 169, 170

Gus Filgate
Page 128

Jeremy Hopley
Page 56

Richard Jung
Page 191

Sandra Lane
Page 188l

David Munns
Page 3l

Pia Tryde
Page 36r

Patrice de Villiers
Page 181